THE RED MOTHER™

VOLUME TWO

Published by

BOOM! STUDIOS™

THE RED MOTHER Volume Two, December 2020. Published by BOOM! Studios, a division of Boom Entertainment, Inc. The Red Mother is ™ & © 2020 Jeremy Haun. Originally published in single magazine form as THE RED MOTHER No. 5-8. ™ & © 2020 Jeremy Haun. All rights reserved. BOOM! Studios™ and the BOOM! Studios logo are trademarks of Boom Entertainment, Inc., registered in various countries and categories. All characters, events, and institutions depicted herein are fictional. Any similarity between any of the names, characters, persons, events, and/or institutions in this publication to actual names, characters, and persons, whether living or dead, events, and/or institutions is unintended and purely coincidental. BOOM! Studios does not read or accept unsolicited submissions of ideas, stories, or artwork.

BOOM! Studios, 5670 Wilshire Boulevard, Suite 400, Los Angeles, CA, 90036-5679. Printed in China. First Printing.

ISBN: 978-1-68415-622-1, eISBN: 978-1-64668-034-4

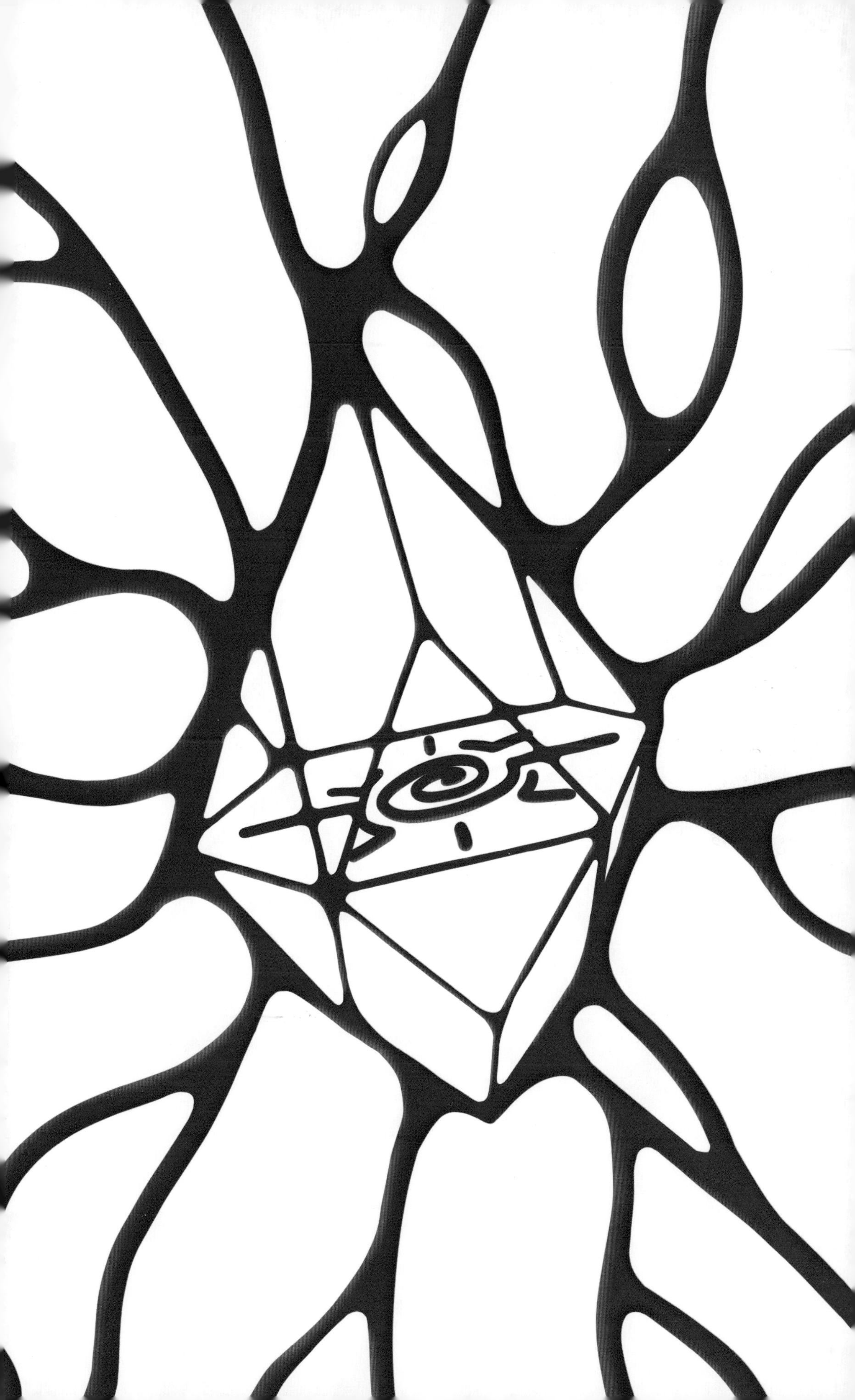

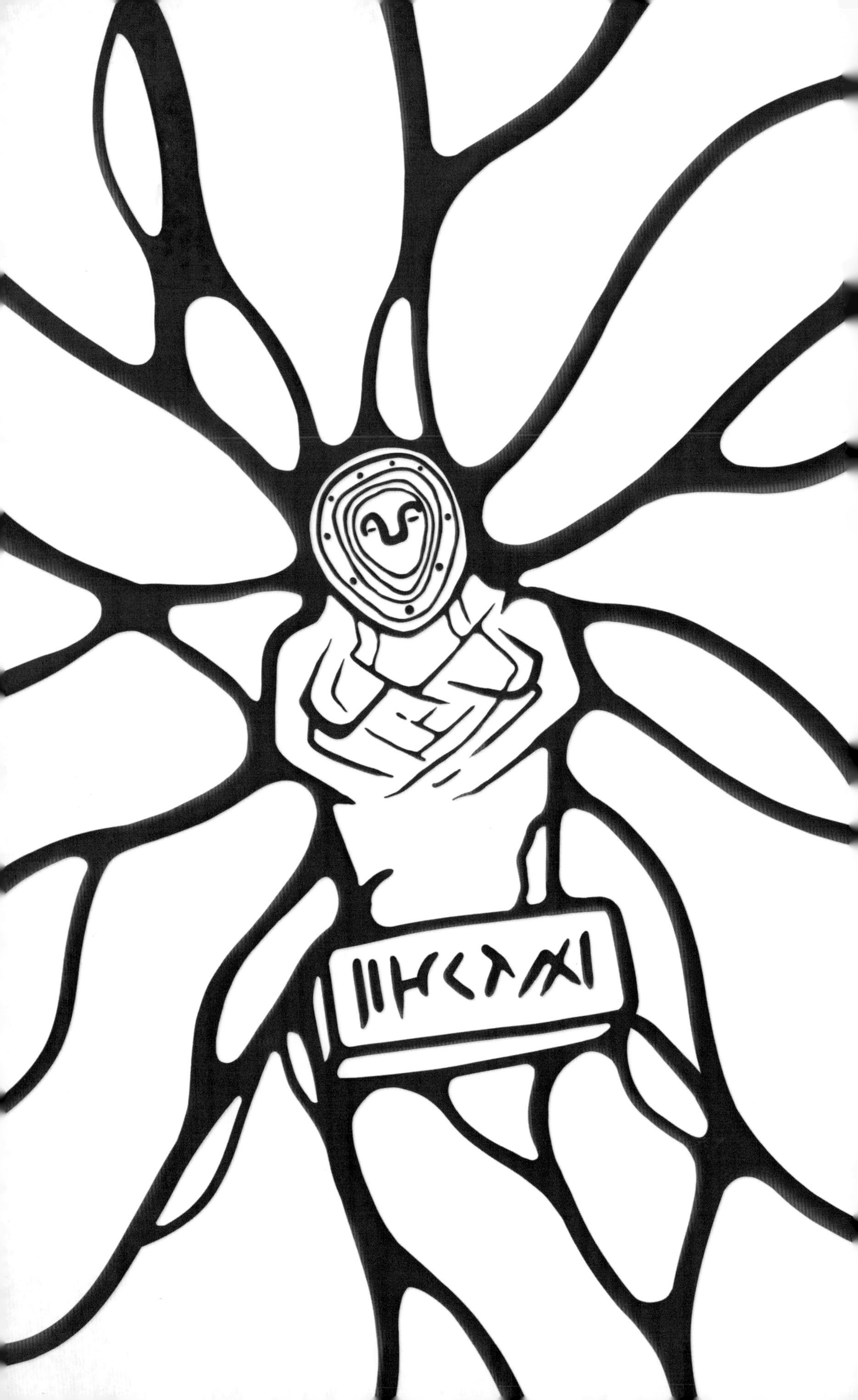

WRITTEN BY
JEREMY HAUN

ILLUSTRATED BY
DANNY LUCKERT

LETTERED BY
ED DUKESHIRE

COVER BY
JEREMY HAUN
WITH COLORS BY **NICK FILARDI**

DESIGNER
MARIE KRUPINA

ASSISTANT EDITORS
RAMIRO PORTNOY
GWEN WALLER

EDITOR
ERIC HARBURN

THE RED MOTHER
CREATED BY **JEREMY HAUN**

CHAPTER
FIVE

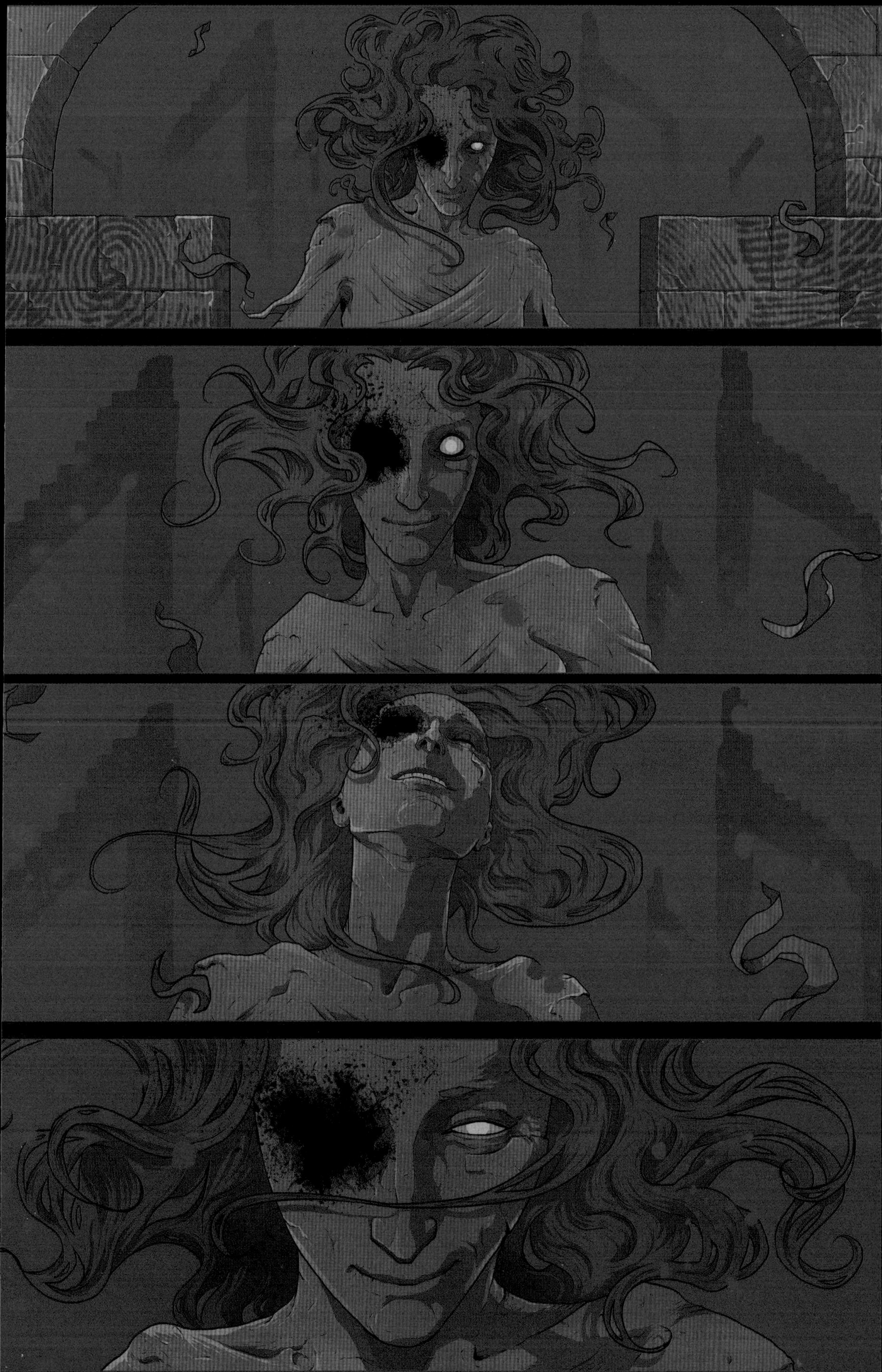

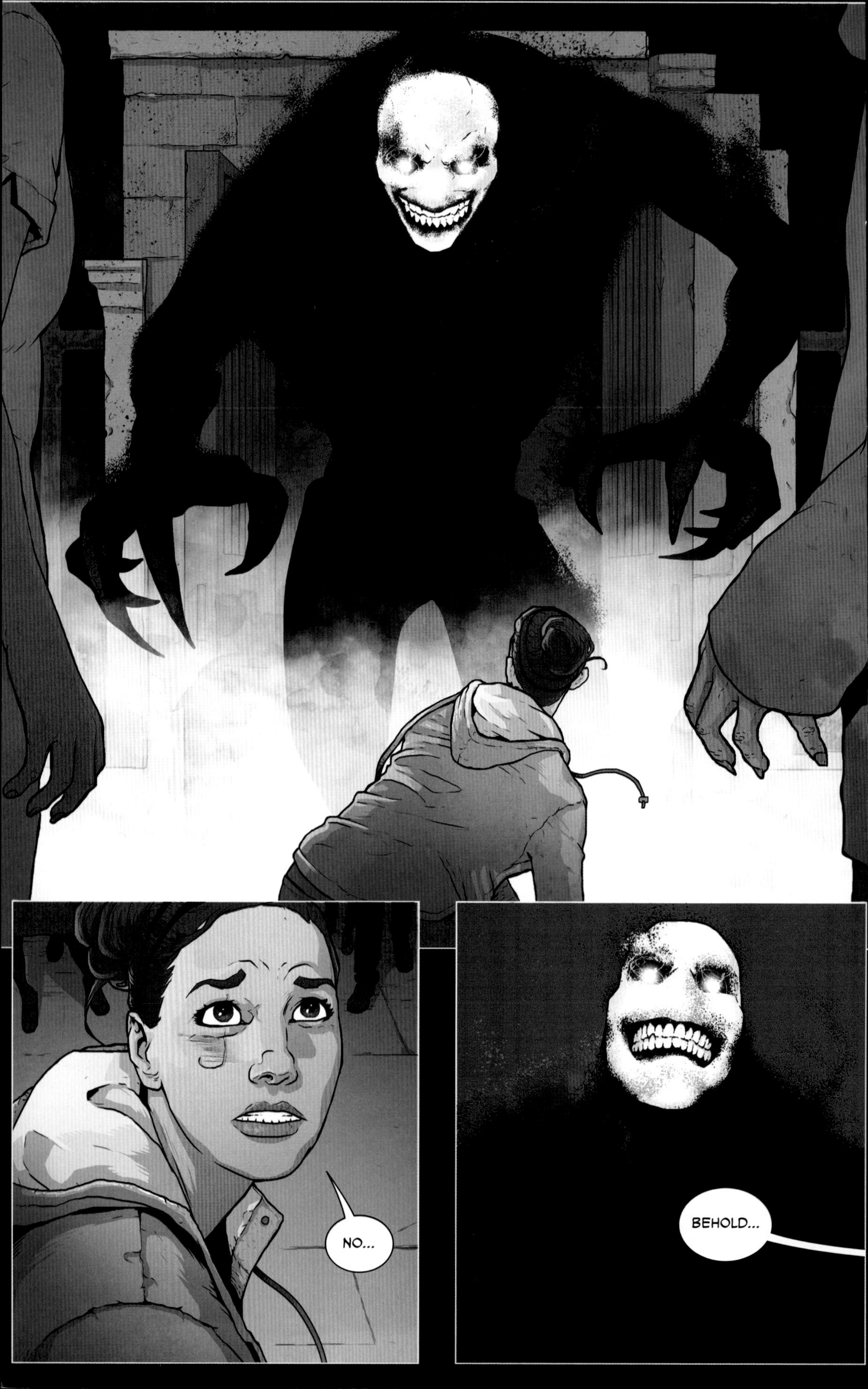
NO...
BEHOLD...

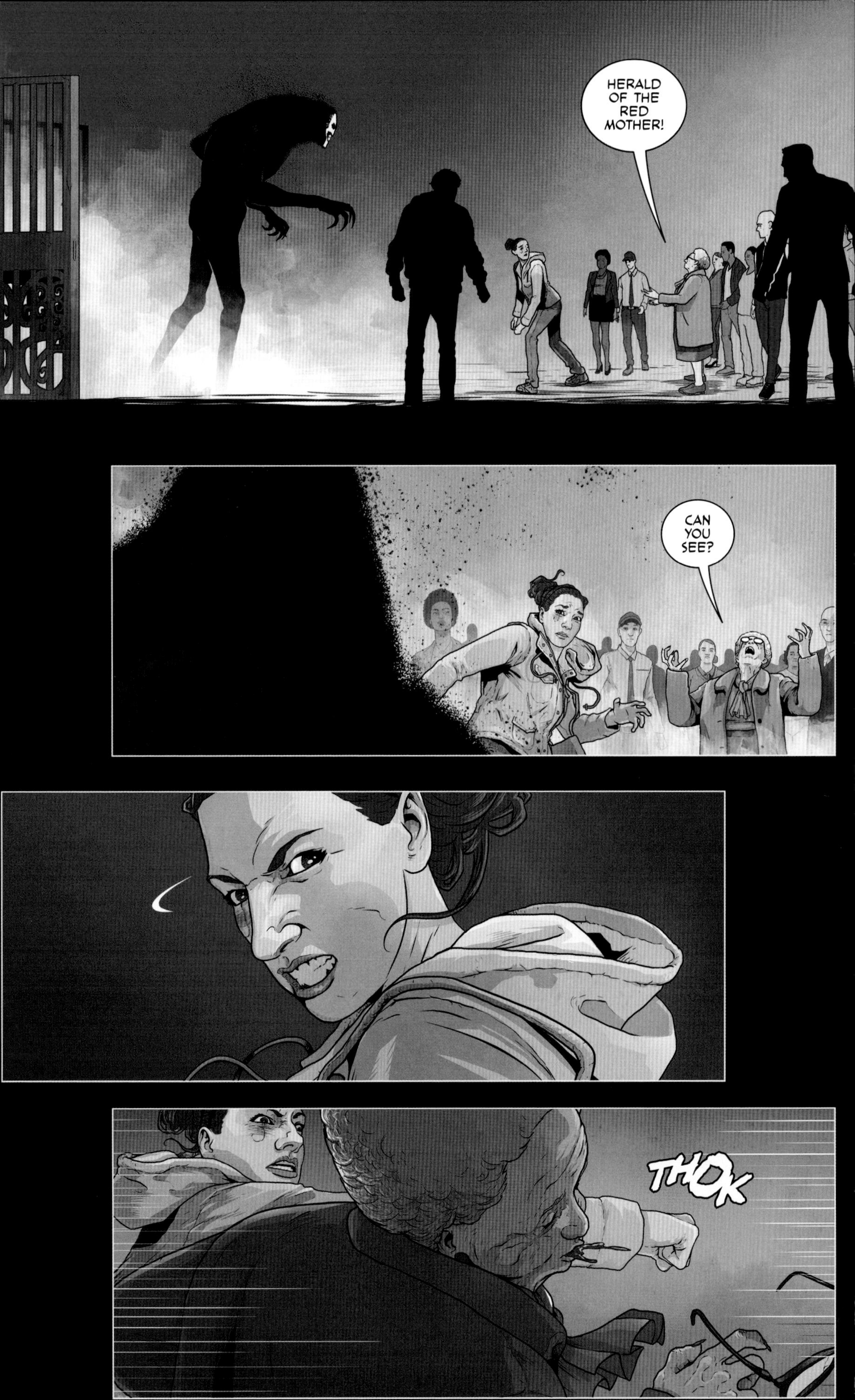
HERALD OF THE RED MOTHER!
CAN YOU SEE?
THOK

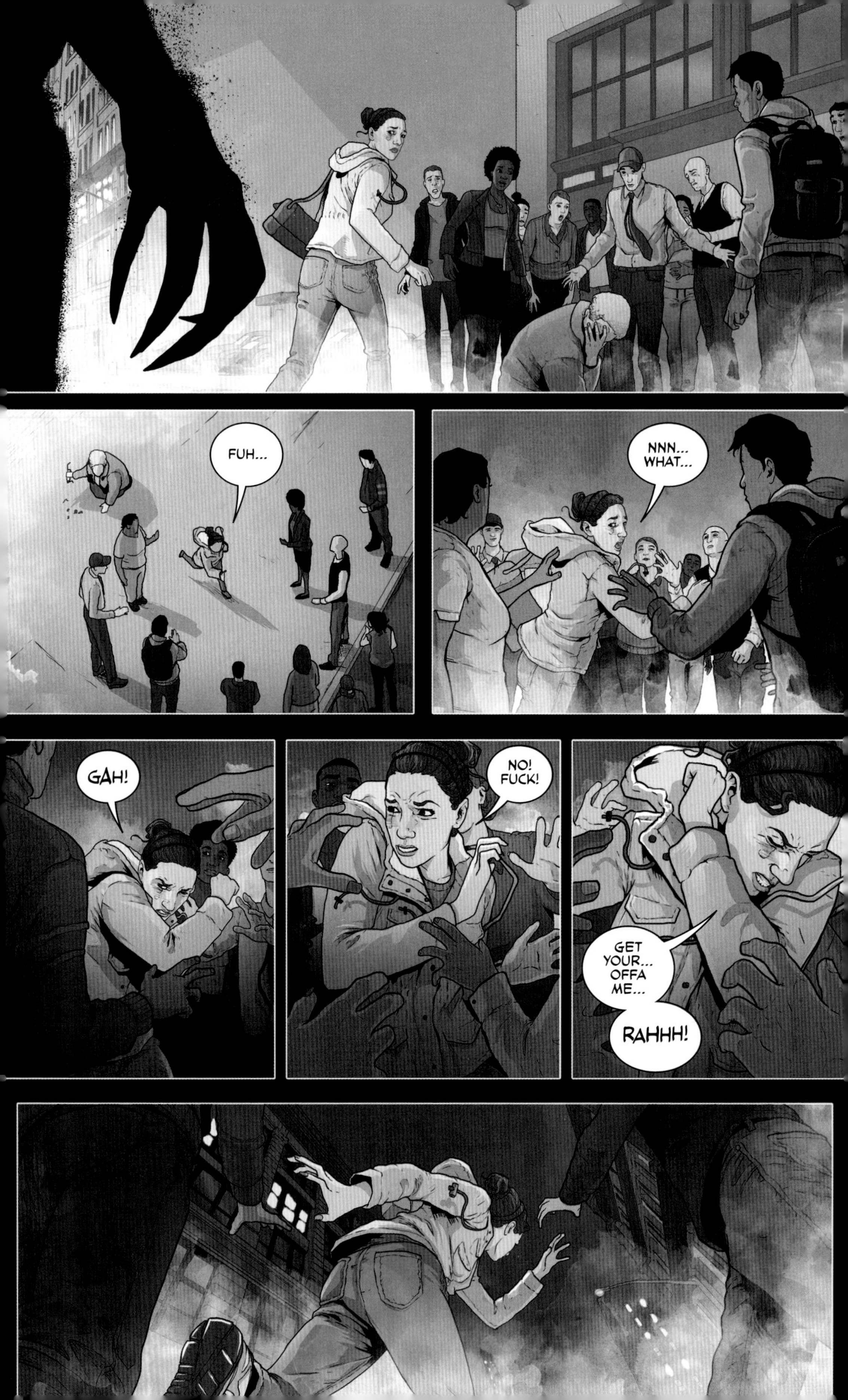
FUH...
NNN... WHAT...
GAH!
NO! FUCK!
GET YOUR... OFFA ME...
RAHHH!

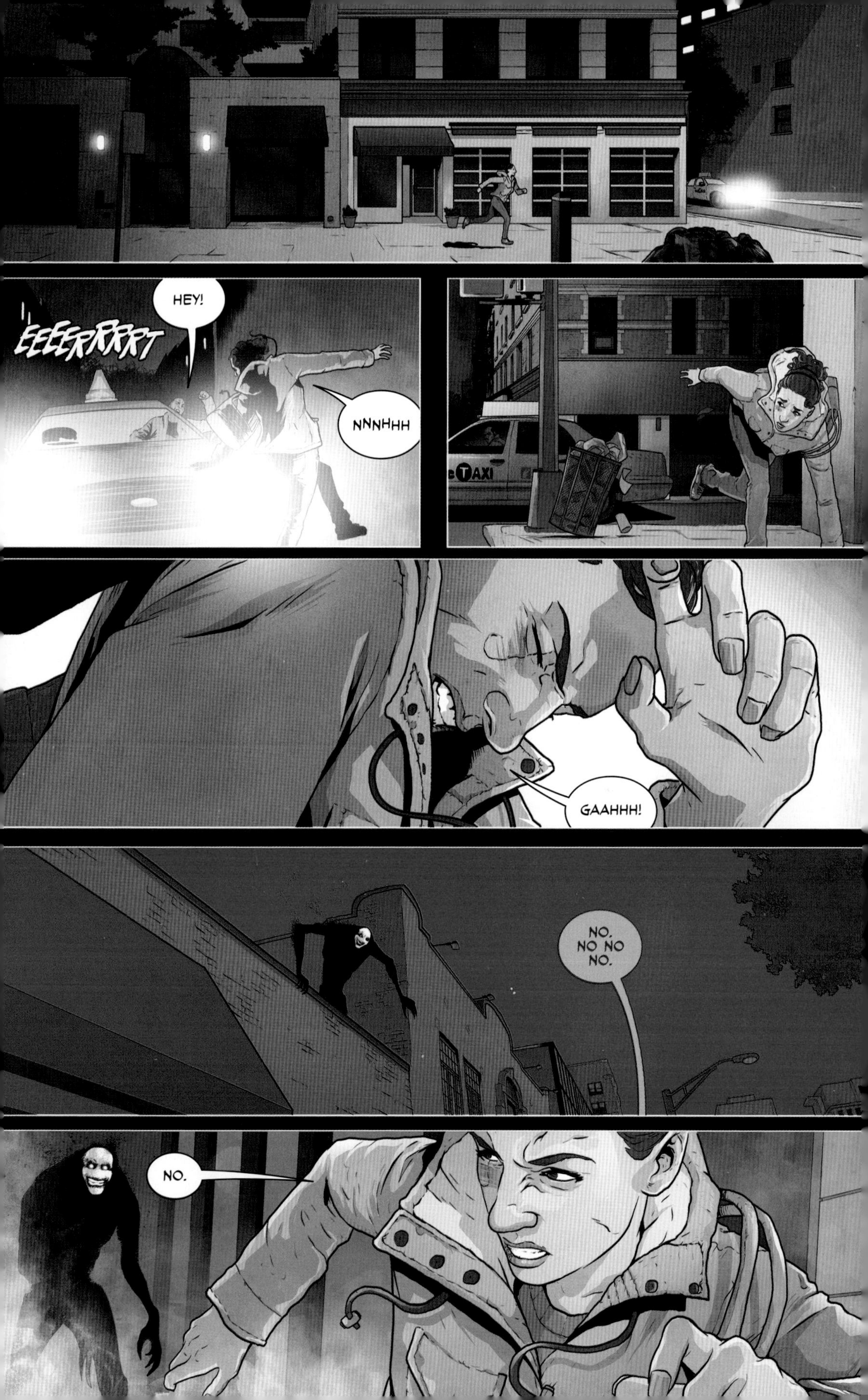
EEEEERRRRRT
HEY!
NNNHHH
TAXI
GAAHHH!
NO. NO NO NO.
NO.

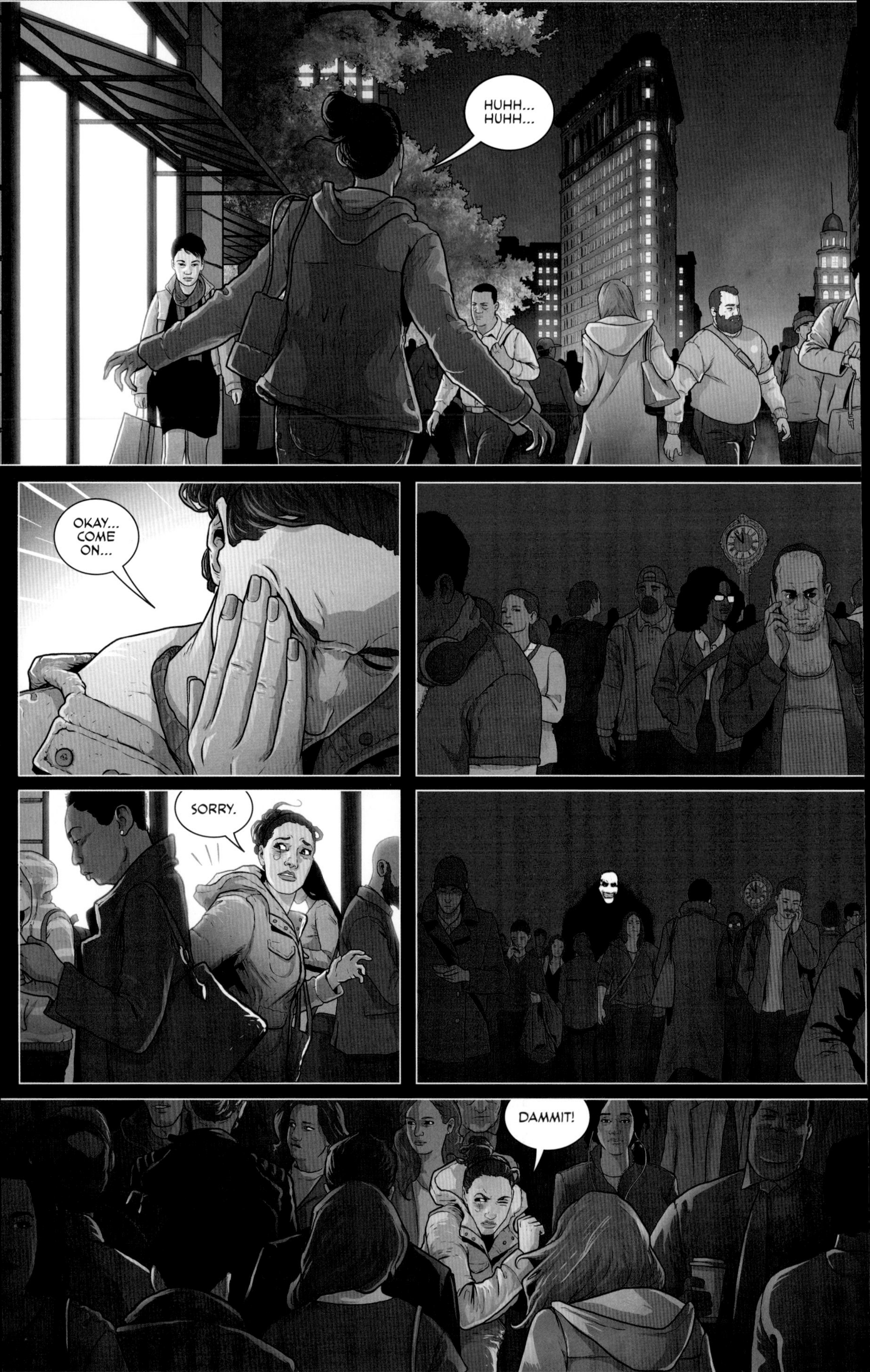
HUHH...
HUHH...
OKAY... COME ON...
SORRY.
DAMMIT!

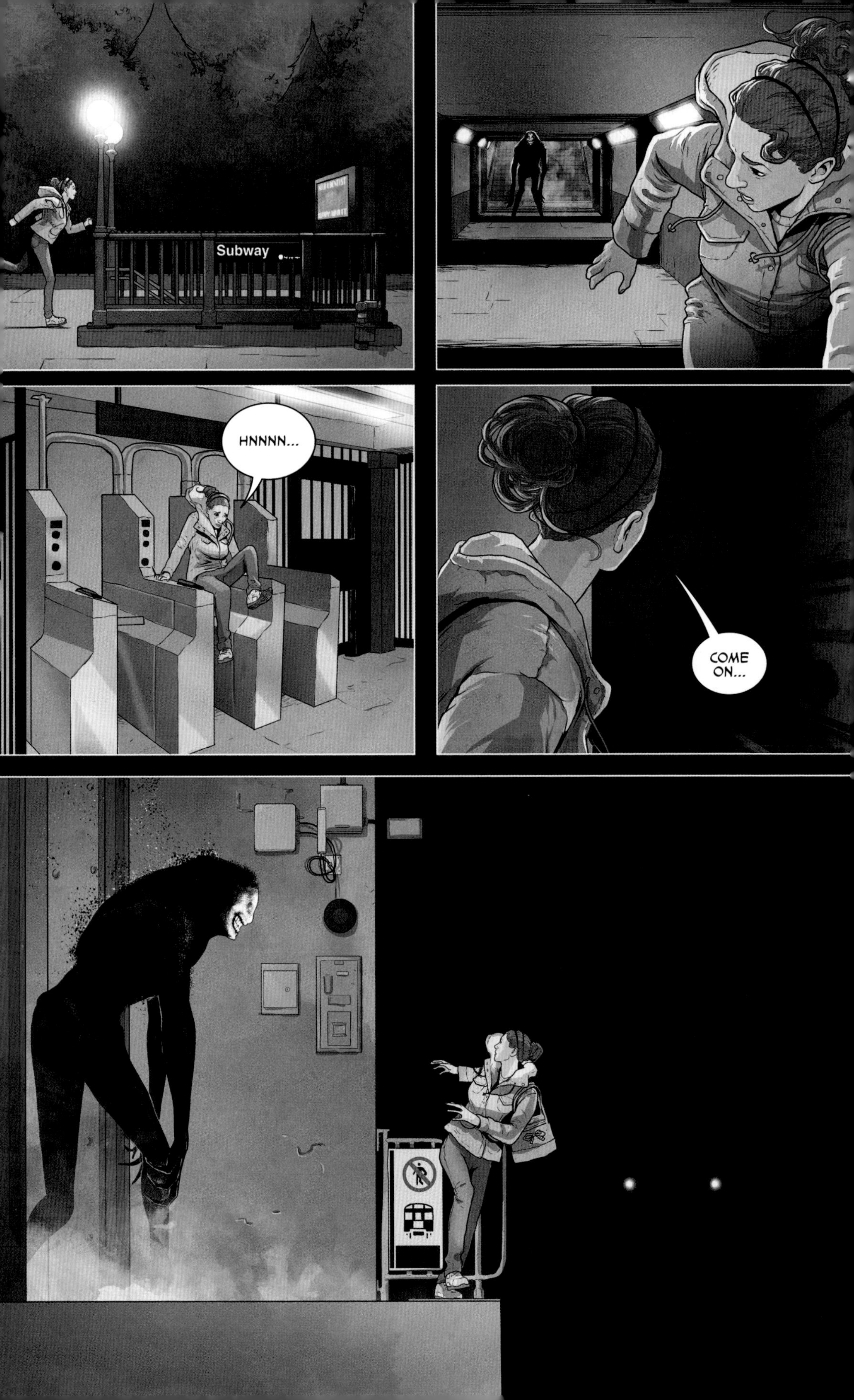
Subway
HNNNN...
COME ON...

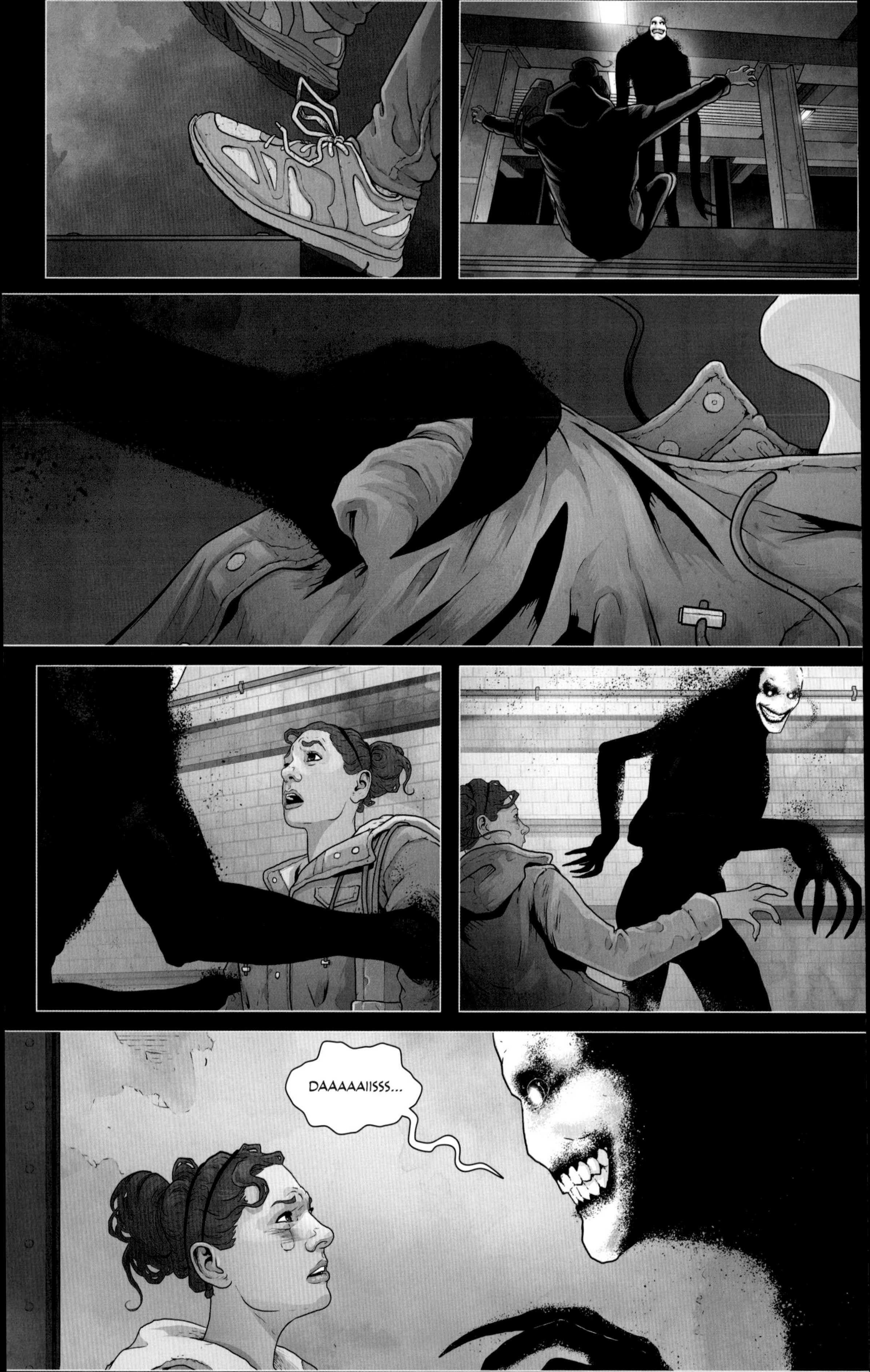
DAAAAAIISSS...

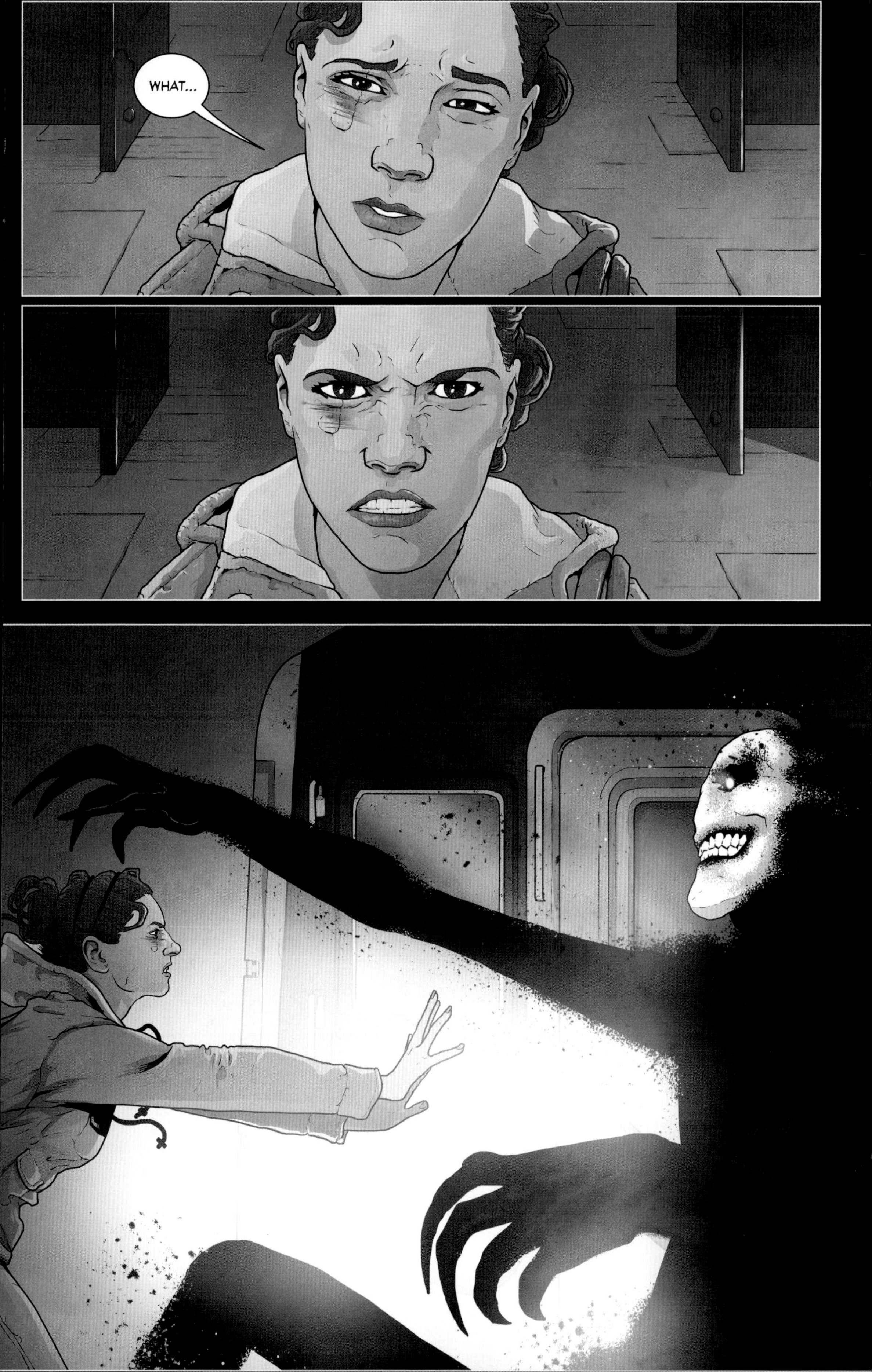
WHAT...

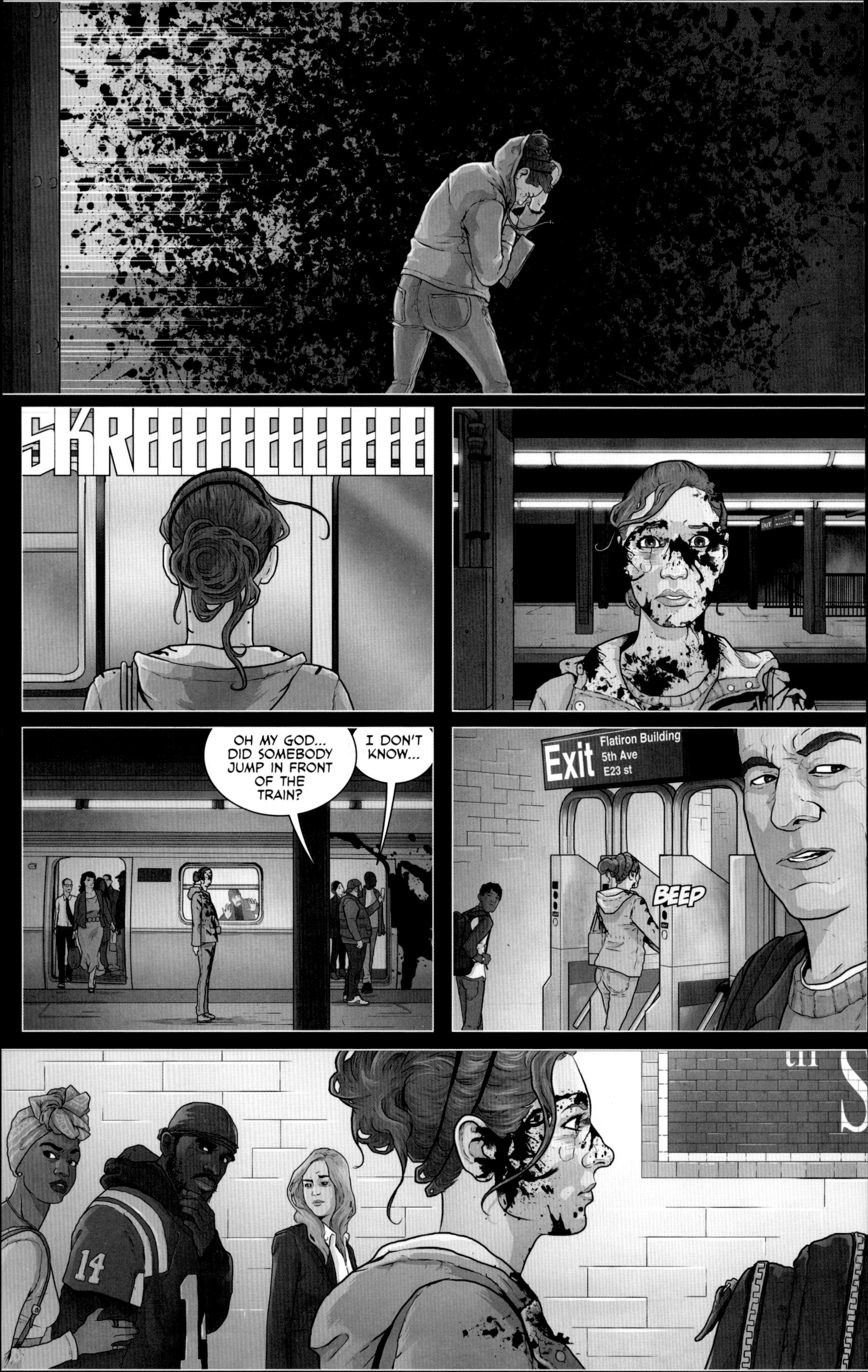
SKREEEEEEEEEEEE
OH MY GOD... DID SOMEBODY JUMP IN FRONT OF THE TRAIN?
I DON'T KNOW...
Exit
Flatiron Building
5th Ave
E23 st
BEEP

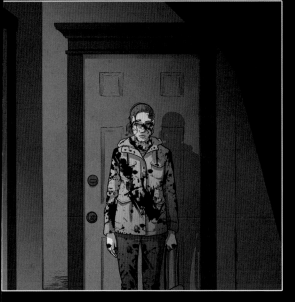

THE RED MOTHER

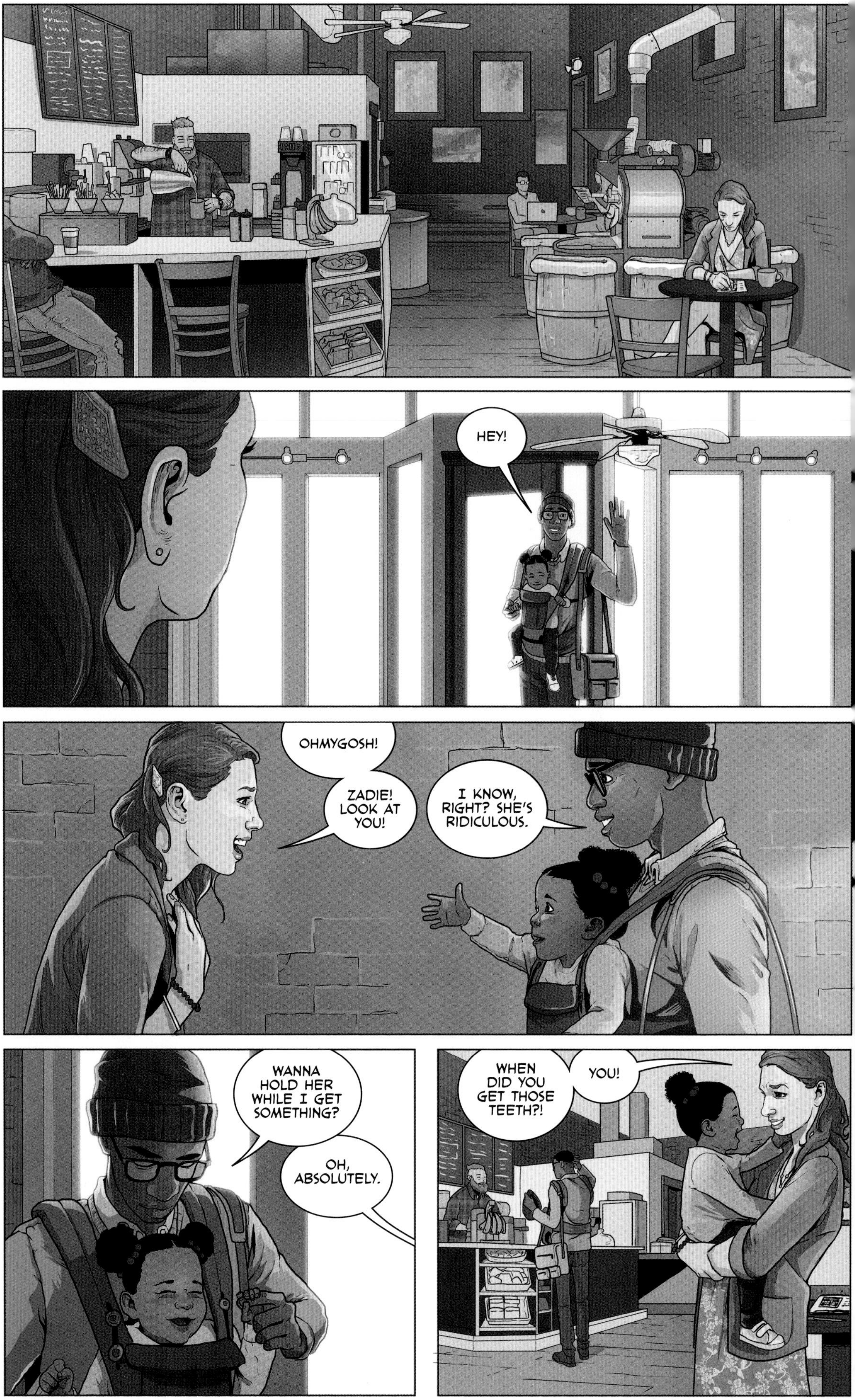
HEY!
OHMYGOSH!
ZADIE! LOOK AT YOU!
I KNOW, RIGHT? SHE'S RIDICULOUS.
WANNA HOLD HER WHILE I GET SOMETHING?
OH, ABSOLUTELY.
WHEN DID YOU GET THOSE TEETH?!
YOU!

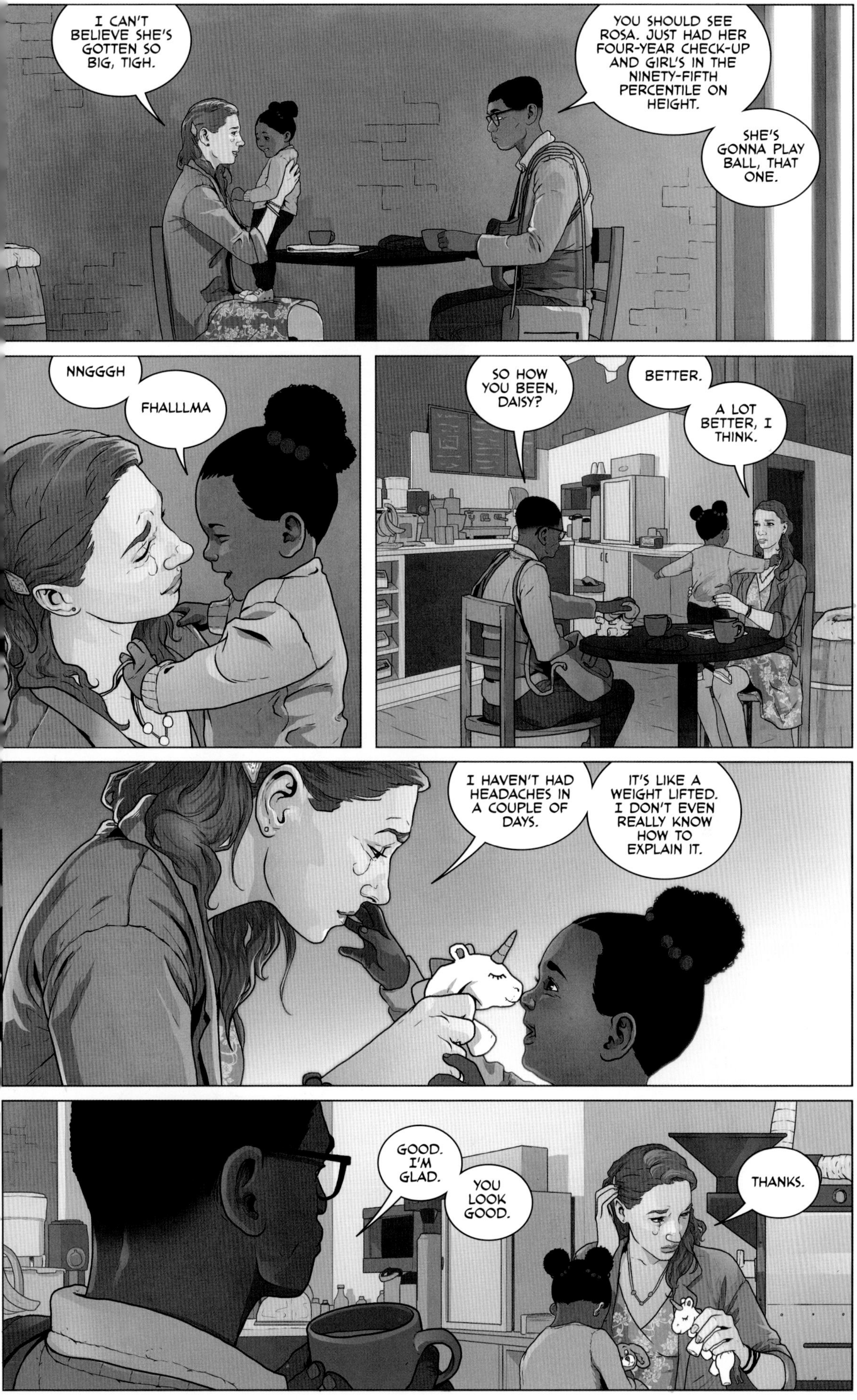
I CAN'T BELIEVE SHE'S GOTTEN SO BIG, TIGH.
YOU SHOULD SEE ROSA. JUST HAD HER FOUR-YEAR CHECK-UP AND GIRL'S IN THE NINETY-FIFTH PERCENTILE ON HEIGHT.
SHE'S GONNA PLAY BALL, THAT ONE.
NNGGGH
FHALLLMA
SO HOW YOU BEEN, DAISY?
BETTER.
A LOT BETTER, I THINK.
I HAVEN'T HAD HEADACHES IN A COUPLE OF DAYS.
IT'S LIKE A WEIGHT LIFTED. I DON'T EVEN REALLY KNOW HOW TO EXPLAIN IT.
GOOD. I'M GLAD.
YOU LOOK GOOD.
THANKS.

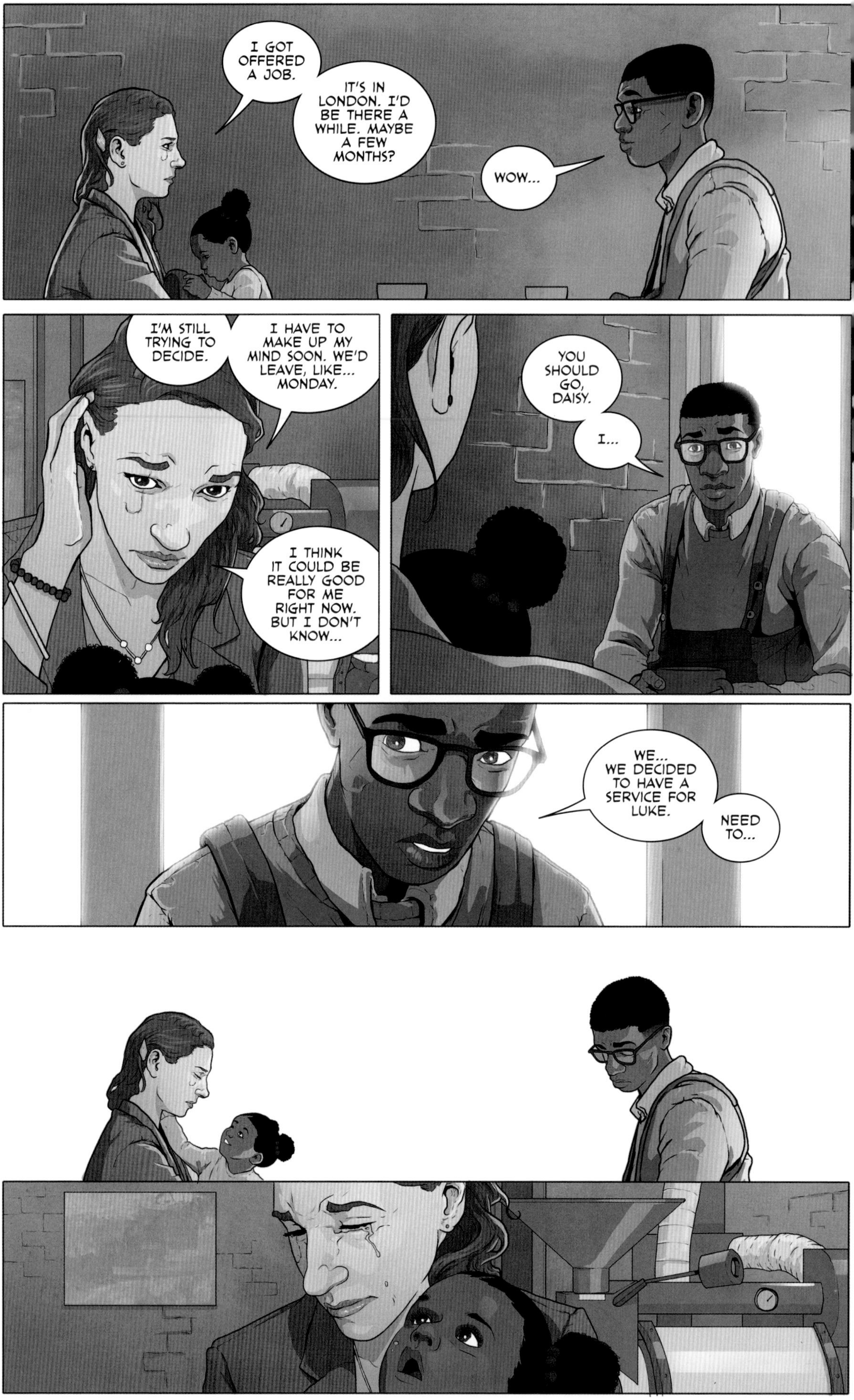
I GOT OFFERED A JOB.
IT'S IN LONDON. I'D BE THERE A WHILE. MAYBE A FEW MONTHS?
WOW...
I'M STILL TRYING TO DECIDE.
I HAVE TO MAKE UP MY MIND SOON. WE'D LEAVE, LIKE... MONDAY.
I THINK IT COULD BE REALLY GOOD FOR ME RIGHT NOW. BUT I DON'T KNOW...
YOU SHOULD GO, DAISY.
I...
WE... WE DECIDED TO HAVE A SERVICE FOR LUKE.
NEED TO...

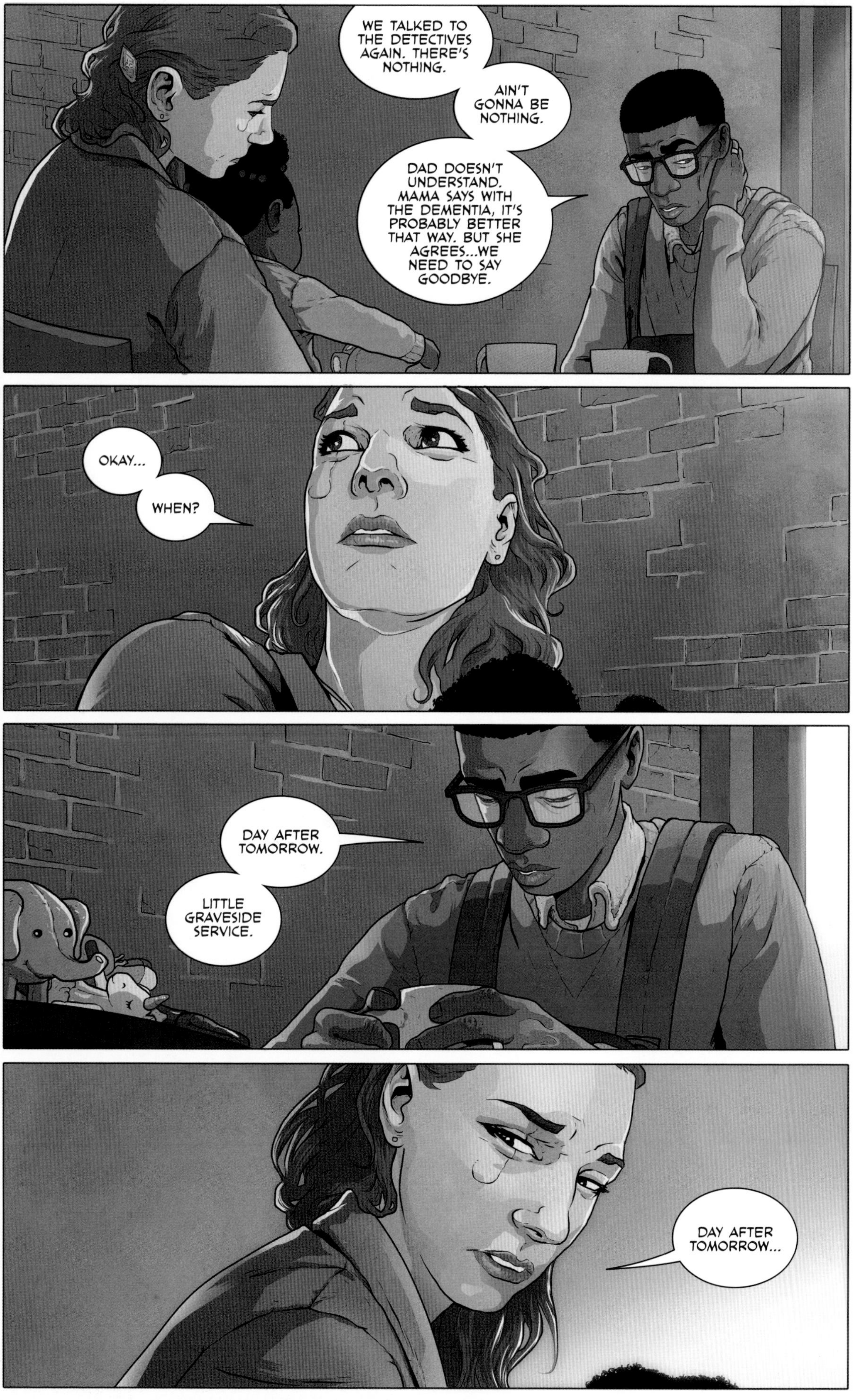
WE TALKED TO THE DETECTIVES AGAIN. THERE'S NOTHING.
AIN'T GONNA BE NOTHING.
DAD DOESN'T UNDERSTAND. MAMA SAYS WITH THE DEMENTIA, IT'S PROBABLY BETTER THAT WAY. BUT SHE AGREES...WE NEED TO SAY GOODBYE.
OKAY...
WHEN?
DAY AFTER TOMORROW.
LITTLE GRAVESIDE SERVICE.
DAY AFTER TOMORROW...

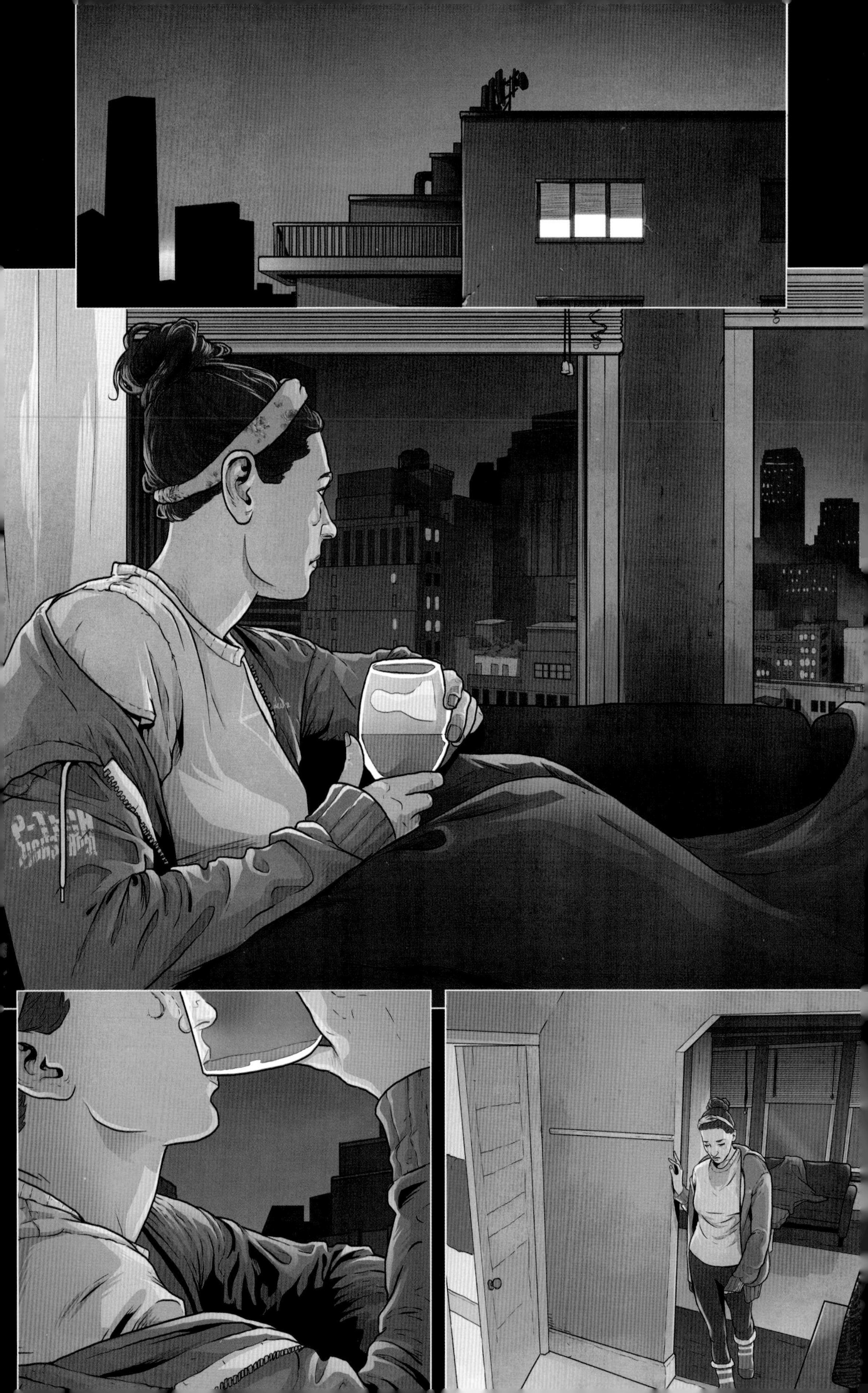

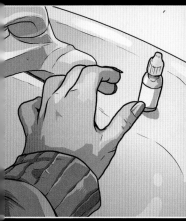

OKAY...

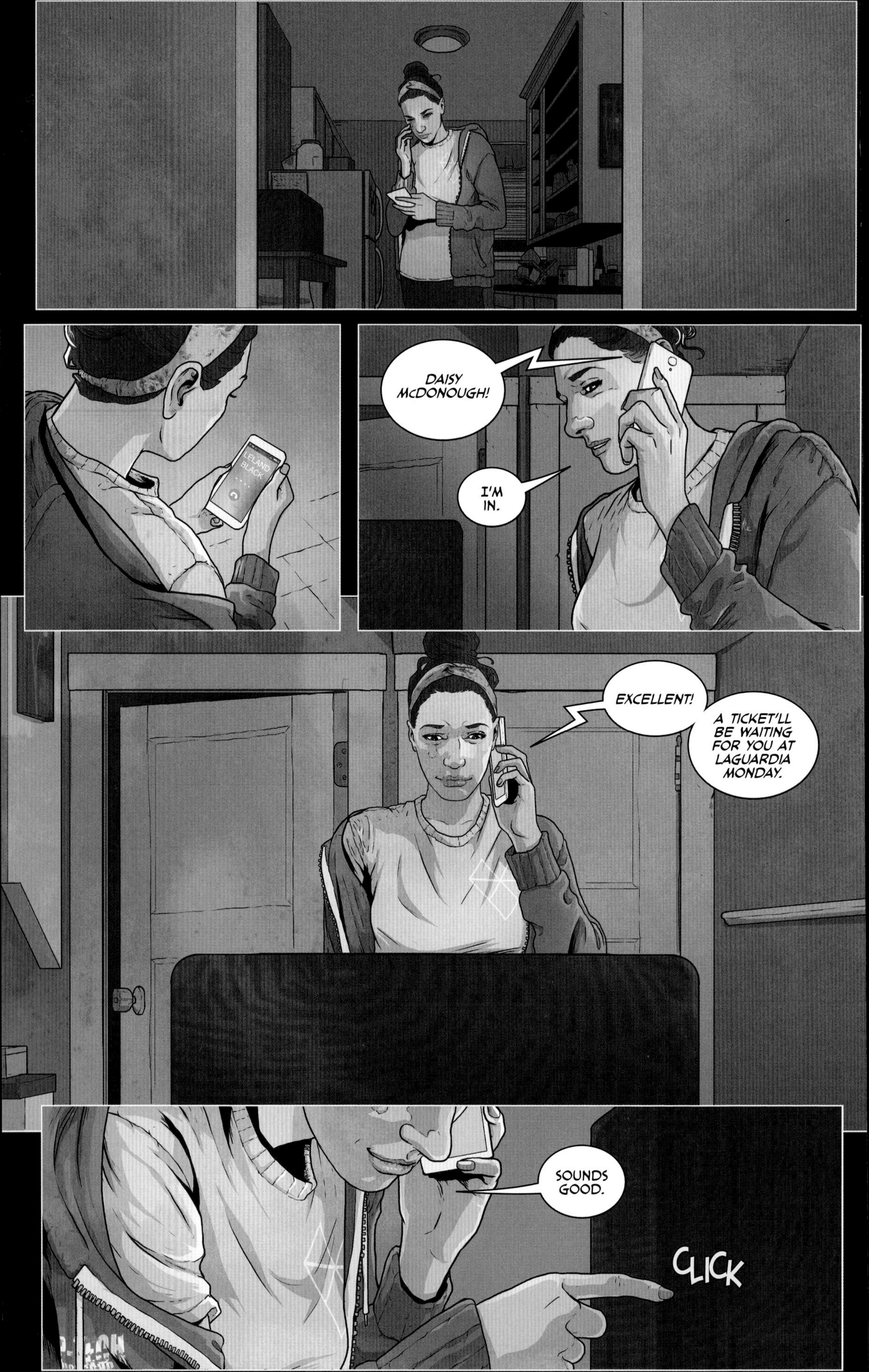
LELAND BLACK
DAISY McDONOUGH!
I'M IN.
EXCELLENT!
A TICKET'LL BE WAITING FOR YOU AT LAGUARDIA MONDAY.
SOUNDS GOOD.
CLICK

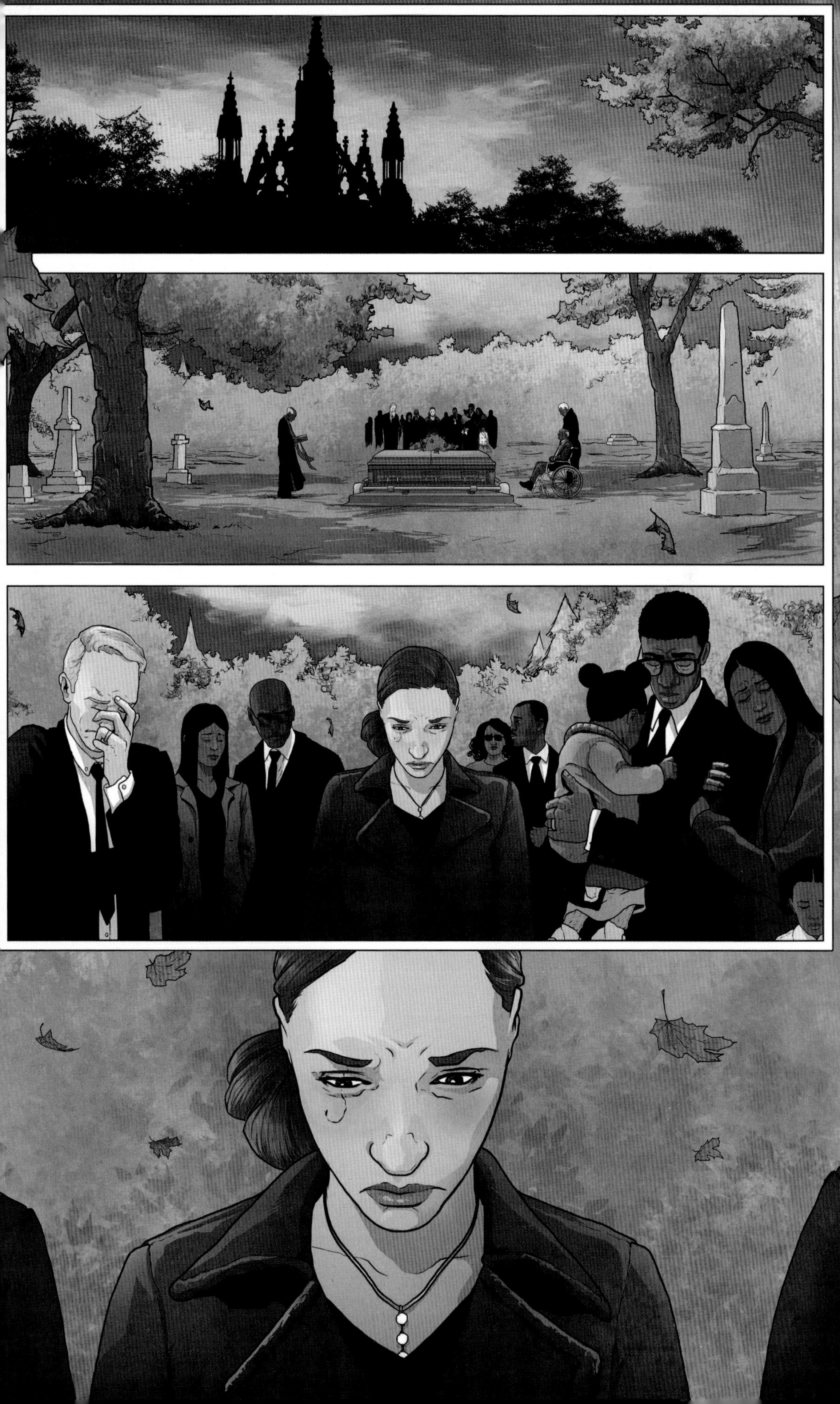

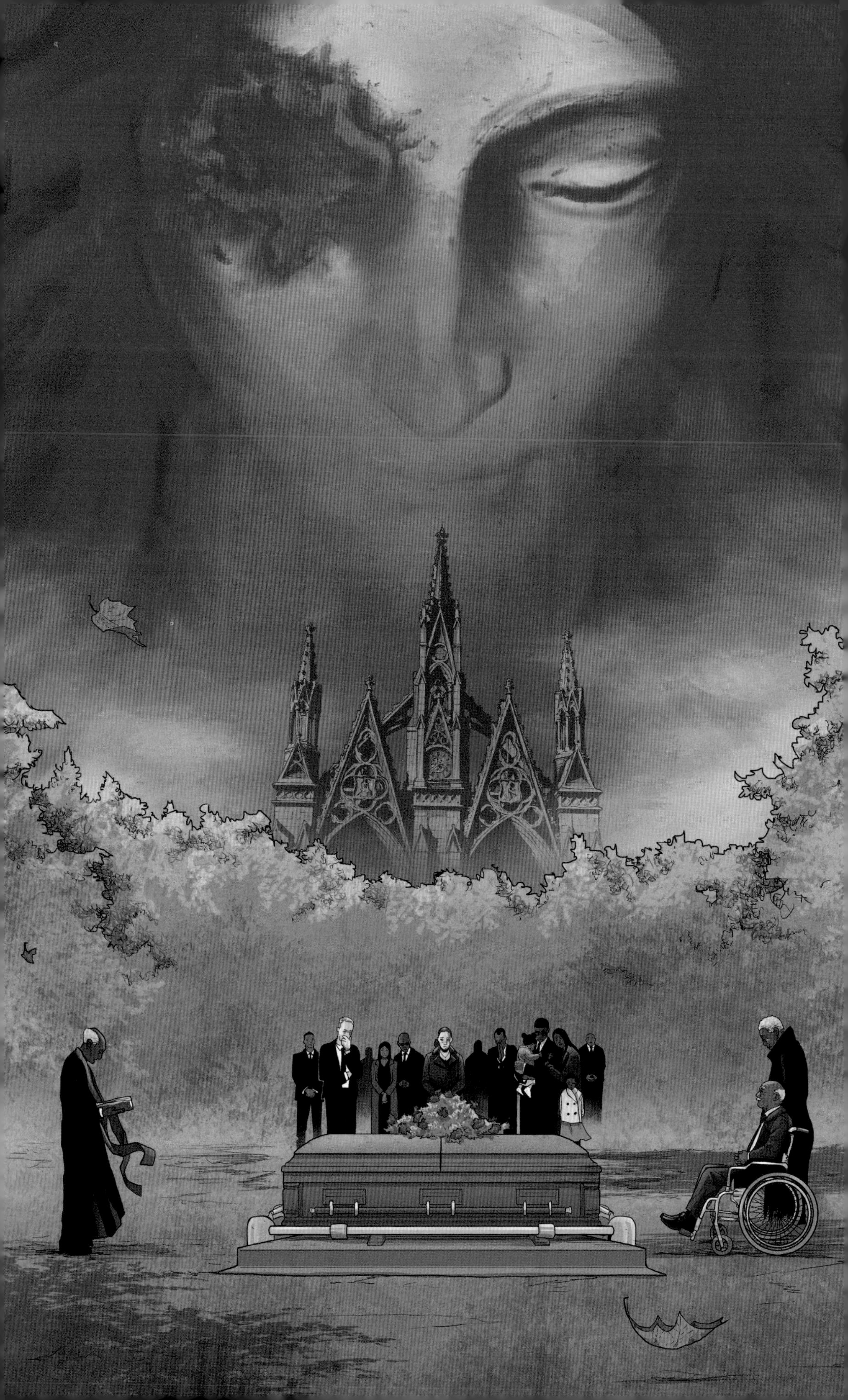

CHAPTER SIX

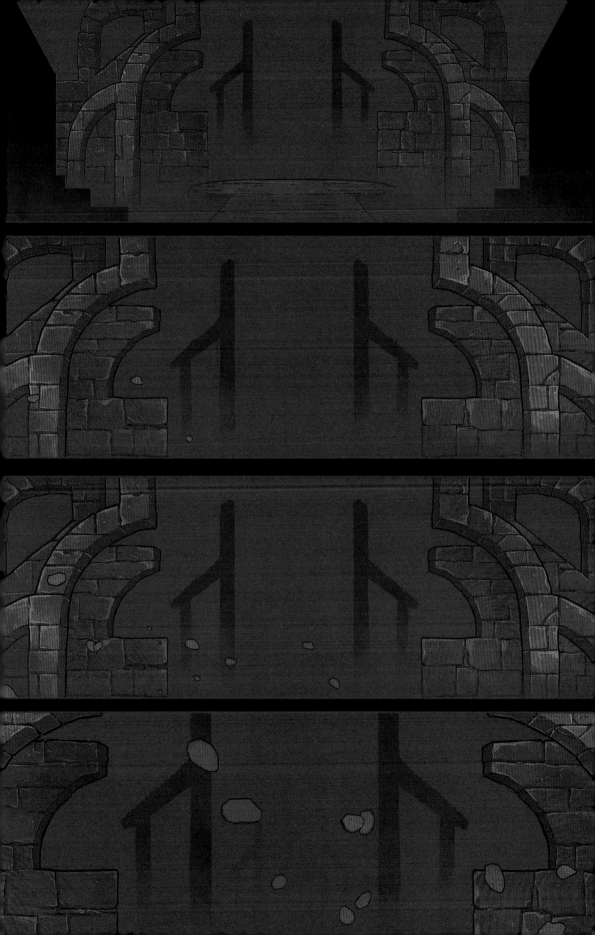

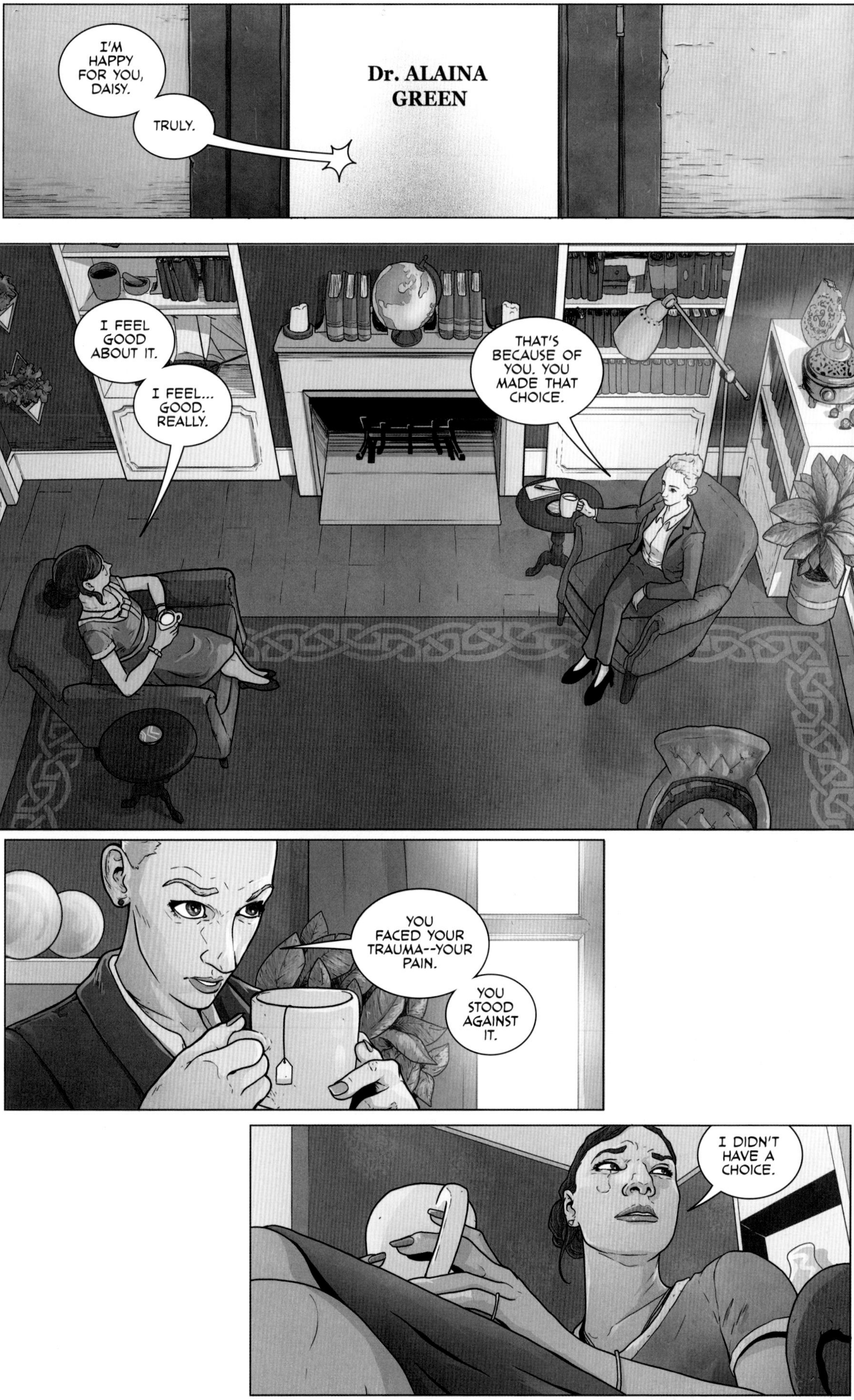
I'M HAPPY FOR YOU, DAISY.
TRULY.
Dr. ALAINA GREEN
I FEEL GOOD ABOUT IT.
I FEEL... GOOD. REALLY.
THAT'S BECAUSE OF YOU. YOU MADE THAT CHOICE.
YOU FACED YOUR TRAUMA--YOUR PAIN.
YOU STOOD AGAINST IT.
I DIDN'T HAVE A CHOICE.

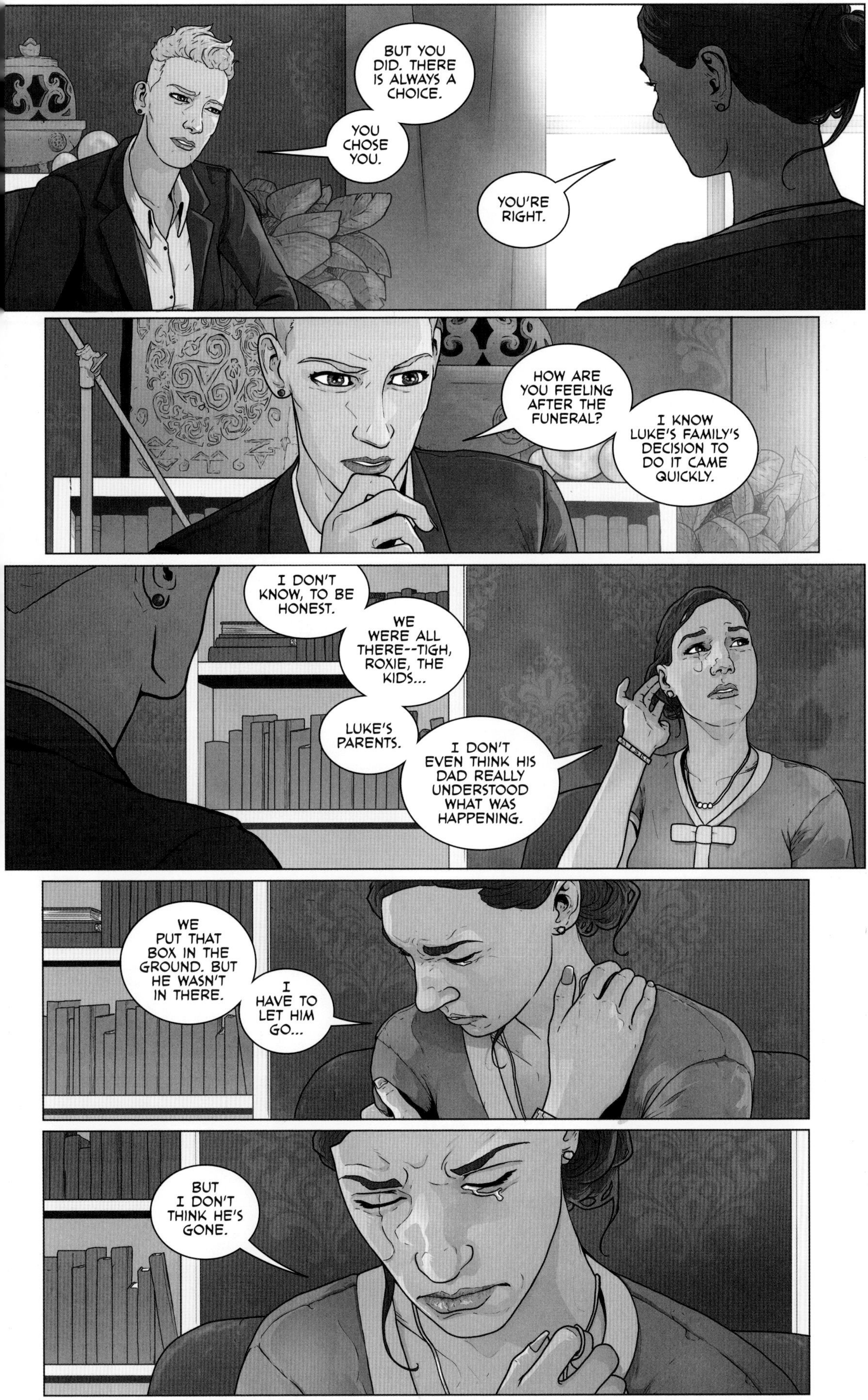
BUT YOU DID. THERE IS ALWAYS A CHOICE.
YOU CHOSE YOU.
YOU'RE RIGHT.
HOW ARE YOU FEELING AFTER THE FUNERAL?
I KNOW LUKE'S FAMILY'S DECISION TO DO IT CAME QUICKLY.
I DON'T KNOW, TO BE HONEST.
WE WERE ALL THERE--TIGH, ROXIE, THE KIDS...
LUKE'S PARENTS.
I DON'T EVEN THINK HIS DAD REALLY UNDERSTOOD WHAT WAS HAPPENING.
WE PUT THAT BOX IN THE GROUND. BUT HE WASN'T IN THERE.
I HAVE TO LET HIM GO...
BUT I DON'T THINK HE'S GONE.

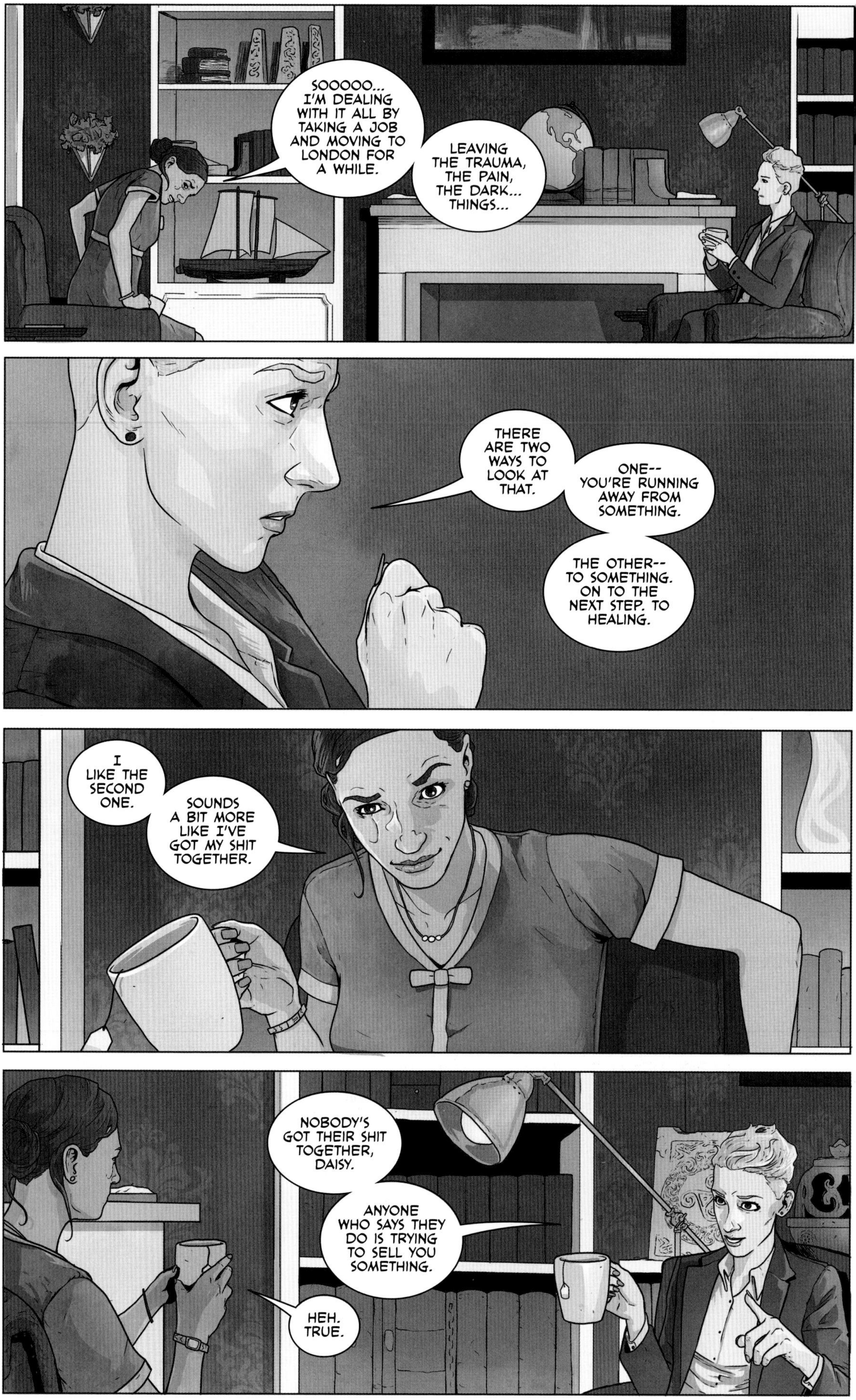
SOOOOO... I'M DEALING WITH IT ALL BY TAKING A JOB AND MOVING TO LONDON FOR A WHILE.
LEAVING THE TRAUMA, THE PAIN, THE DARK... THINGS...
THERE ARE TWO WAYS TO LOOK AT THAT.
ONE-- YOU'RE RUNNING AWAY FROM SOMETHING.
THE OTHER-- TO SOMETHING. ON TO THE NEXT STEP. TO HEALING.
I LIKE THE SECOND ONE.
SOUNDS A BIT MORE LIKE I'VE GOT MY SHIT TOGETHER.
NOBODY'S GOT THEIR SHIT TOGETHER, DAISY.
ANYONE WHO SAYS THEY DO IS TRYING TO SELL YOU SOMETHING.
HEH. TRUE.

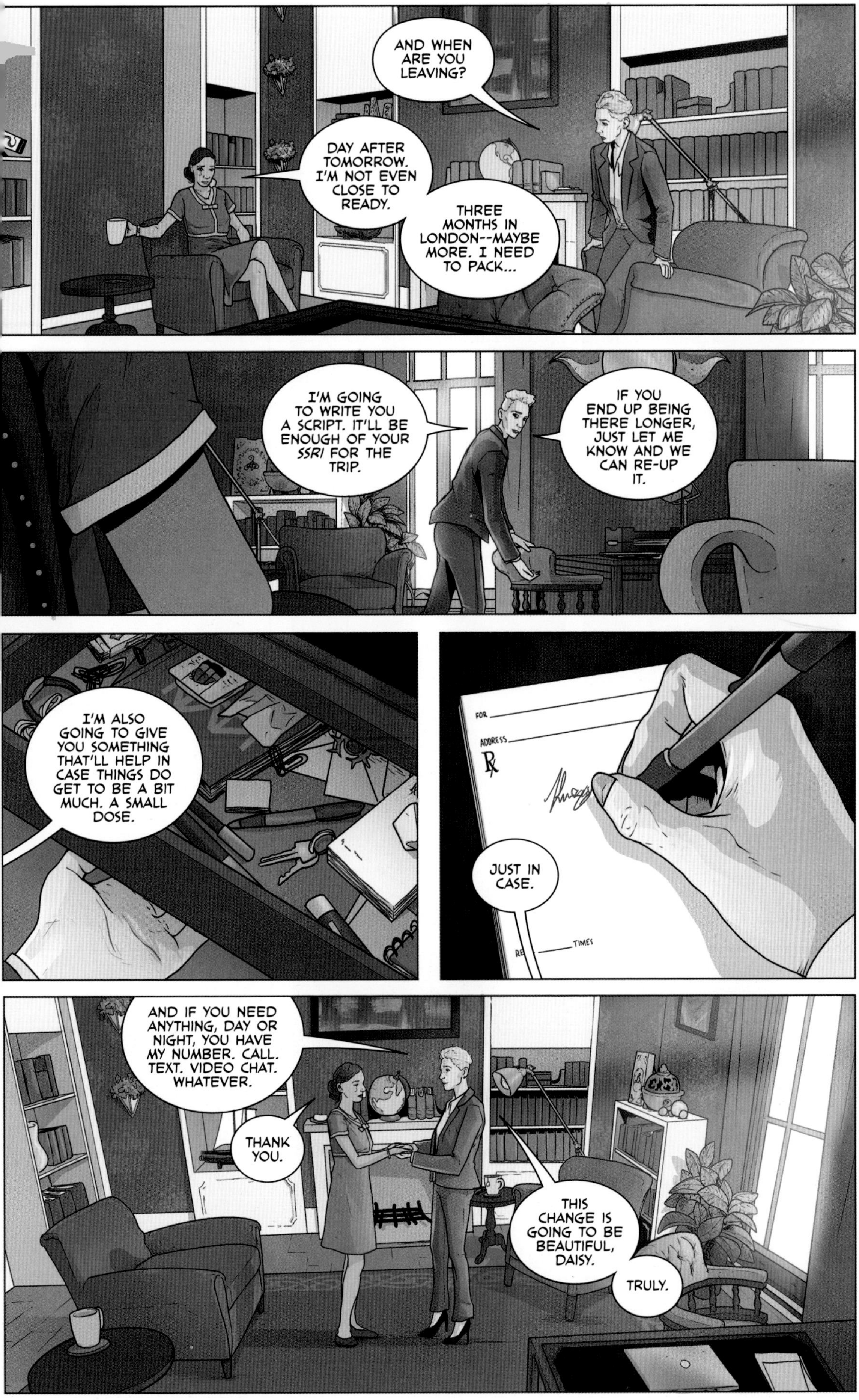
AND WHEN ARE YOU LEAVING?
DAY AFTER TOMORROW. I'M NOT EVEN CLOSE TO READY.
THREE MONTHS IN LONDON--MAYBE MORE. I NEED TO PACK...
I'M GOING TO WRITE YOU A SCRIPT. IT'LL BE ENOUGH OF YOUR SSRI FOR THE TRIP.
IF YOU END UP BEING THERE LONGER, JUST LET ME KNOW AND WE CAN RE-UP IT.
I'M ALSO GOING TO GIVE YOU SOMETHING THAT'LL HELP IN CASE THINGS DO GET TO BE A BIT MUCH. A SMALL DOSE.
FOR
ADDRESS
℞
JUST IN CASE.
TIMES
AND IF YOU NEED ANYTHING, DAY OR NIGHT, YOU HAVE MY NUMBER. CALL. TEXT. VIDEO CHAT. WHATEVER.
THANK YOU.
THIS CHANGE IS GOING TO BE BEAUTIFUL, DAISY.
TRULY.

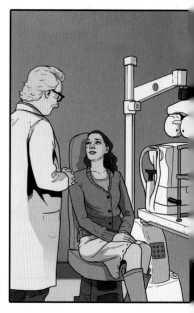

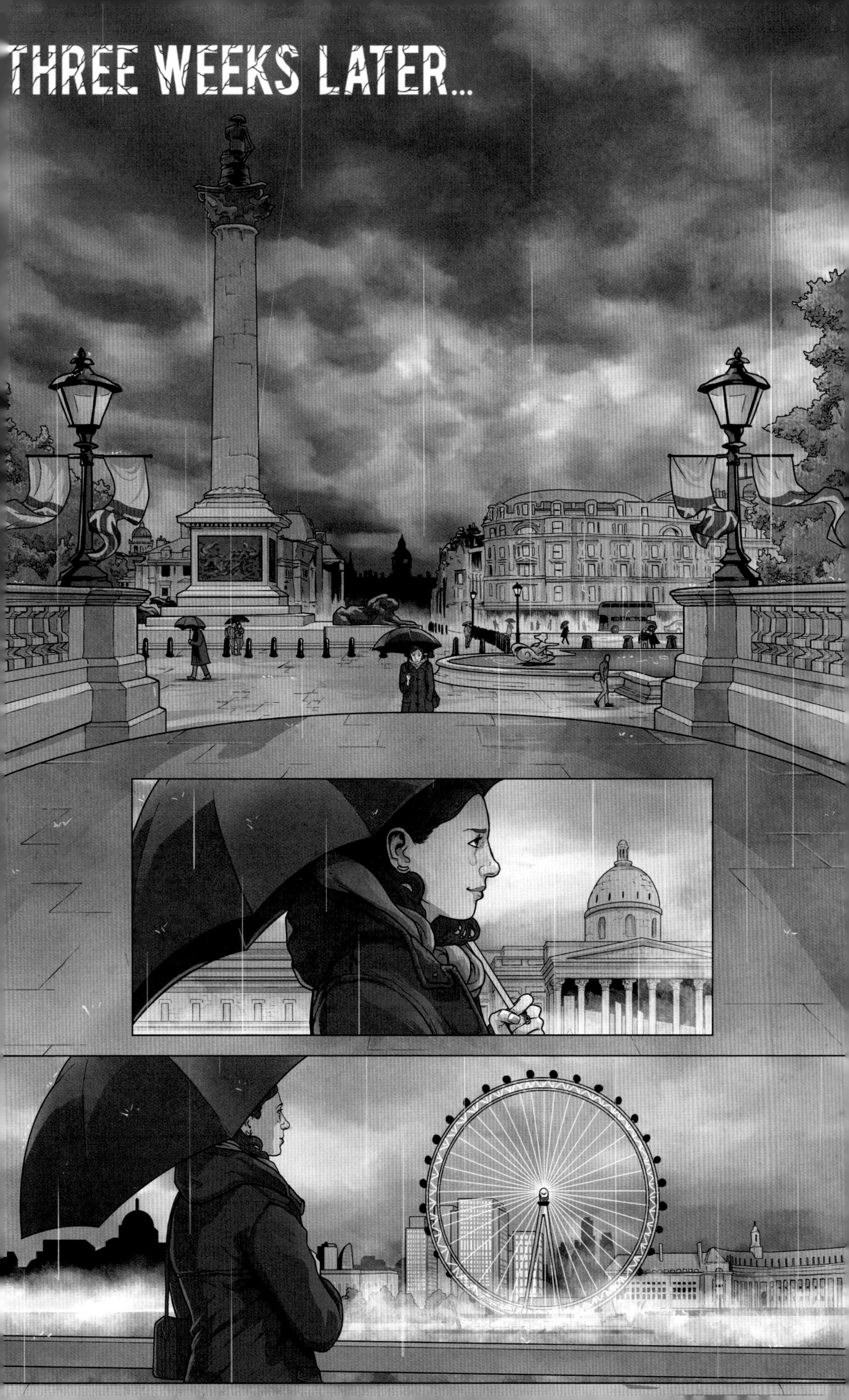
THREE WEEKS LATER...

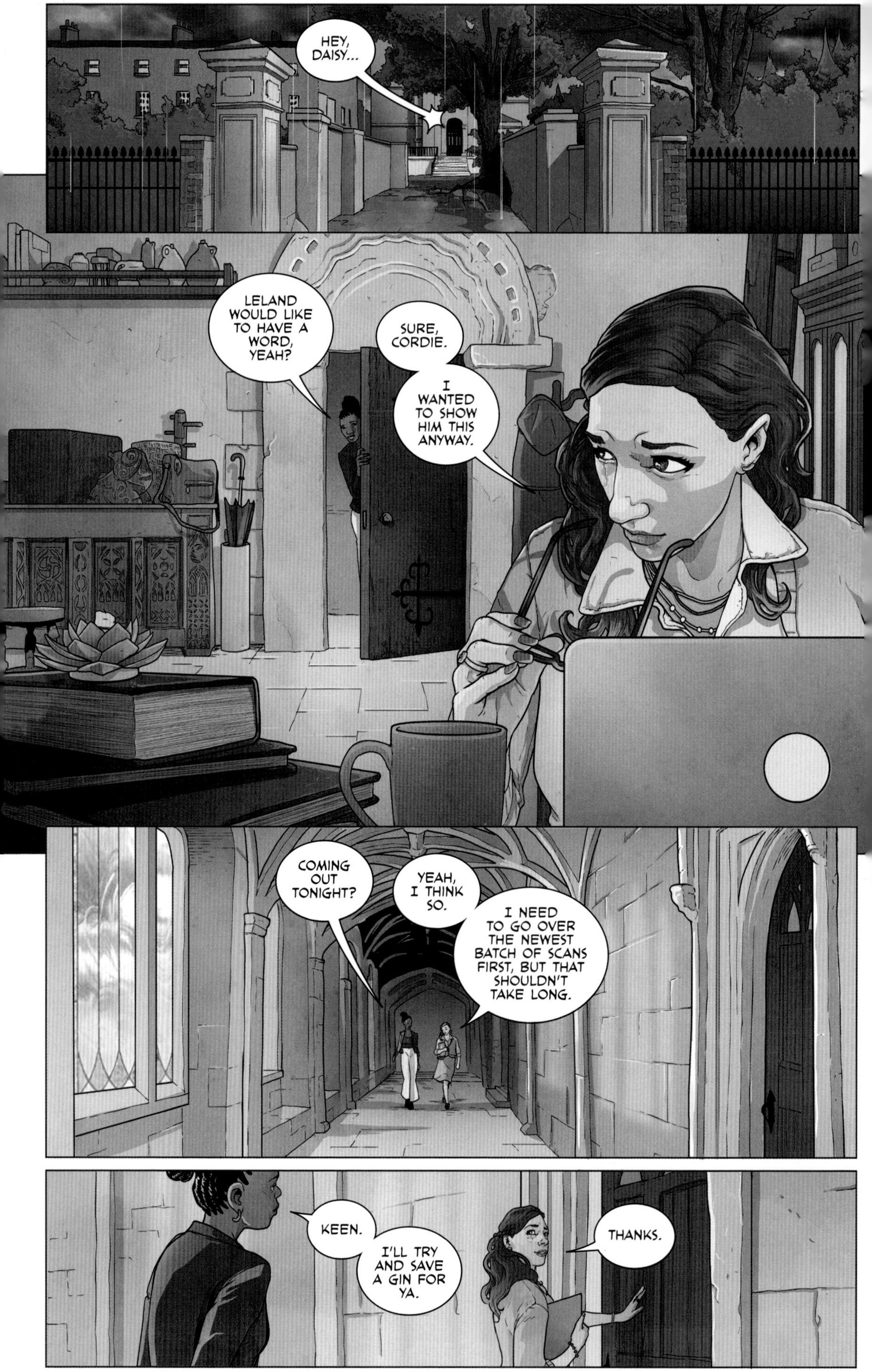
HEY, DAISY...
LELAND WOULD LIKE TO HAVE A WORD, YEAH?
SURE, CORDIE.
I WANTED TO SHOW HIM THIS ANYWAY.
COMING OUT TONIGHT?
YEAH, I THINK SO.
I NEED TO GO OVER THE NEWEST BATCH OF SCANS FIRST, BUT THAT SHOULDN'T TAKE LONG.
KEEN.
I'LL TRY AND SAVE A GIN FOR YA.
THANKS.

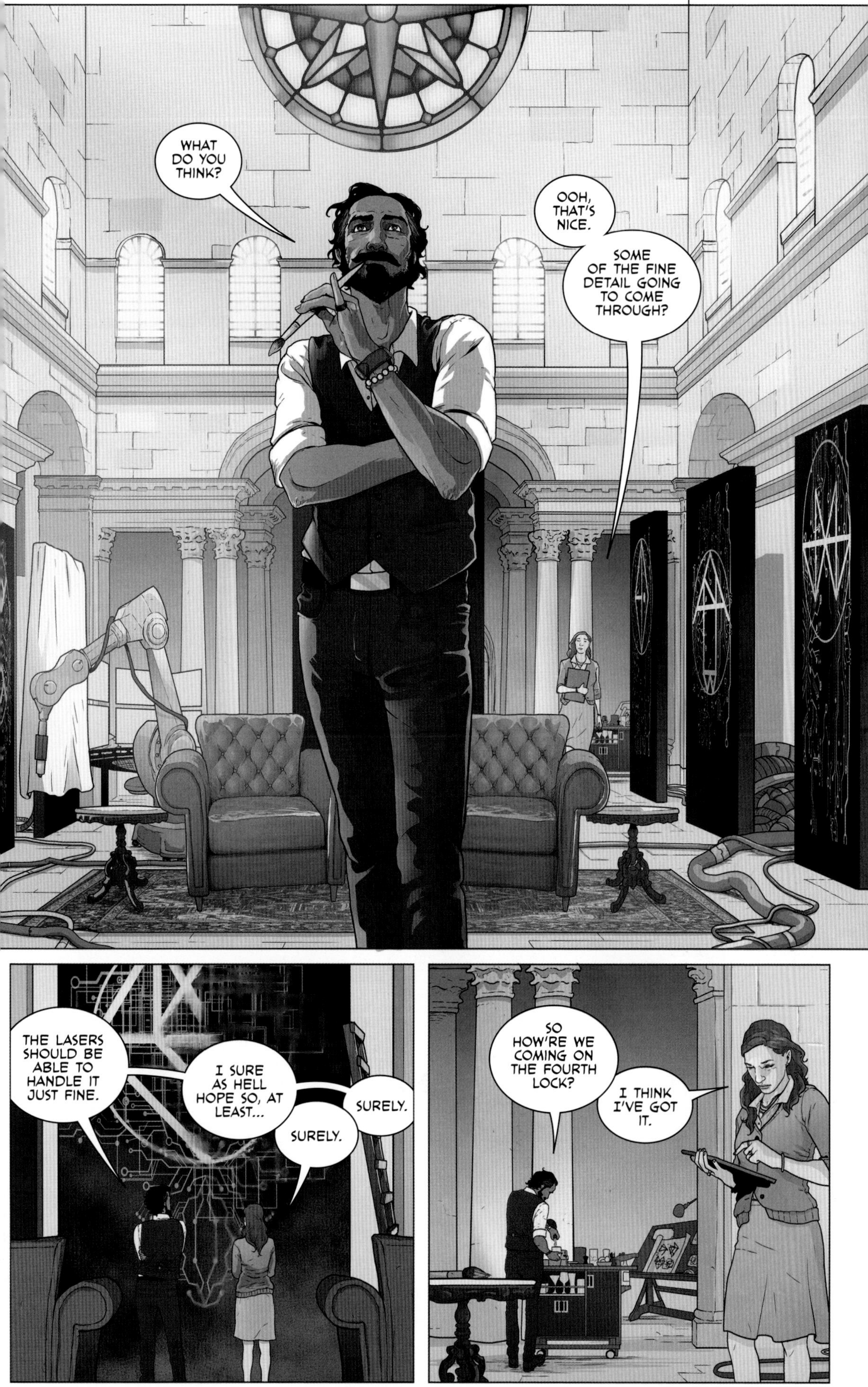
WHAT DO YOU THINK?
OOH, THAT'S NICE.
SOME OF THE FINE DETAIL GOING TO COME THROUGH?
THE LASERS SHOULD BE ABLE TO HANDLE IT JUST FINE.
I SURE AS HELL HOPE SO, AT LEAST...
SURELY.
SURELY.
SO HOW'RE WE COMING ON THE FOURTH LOCK?
I THINK I'VE GOT IT.

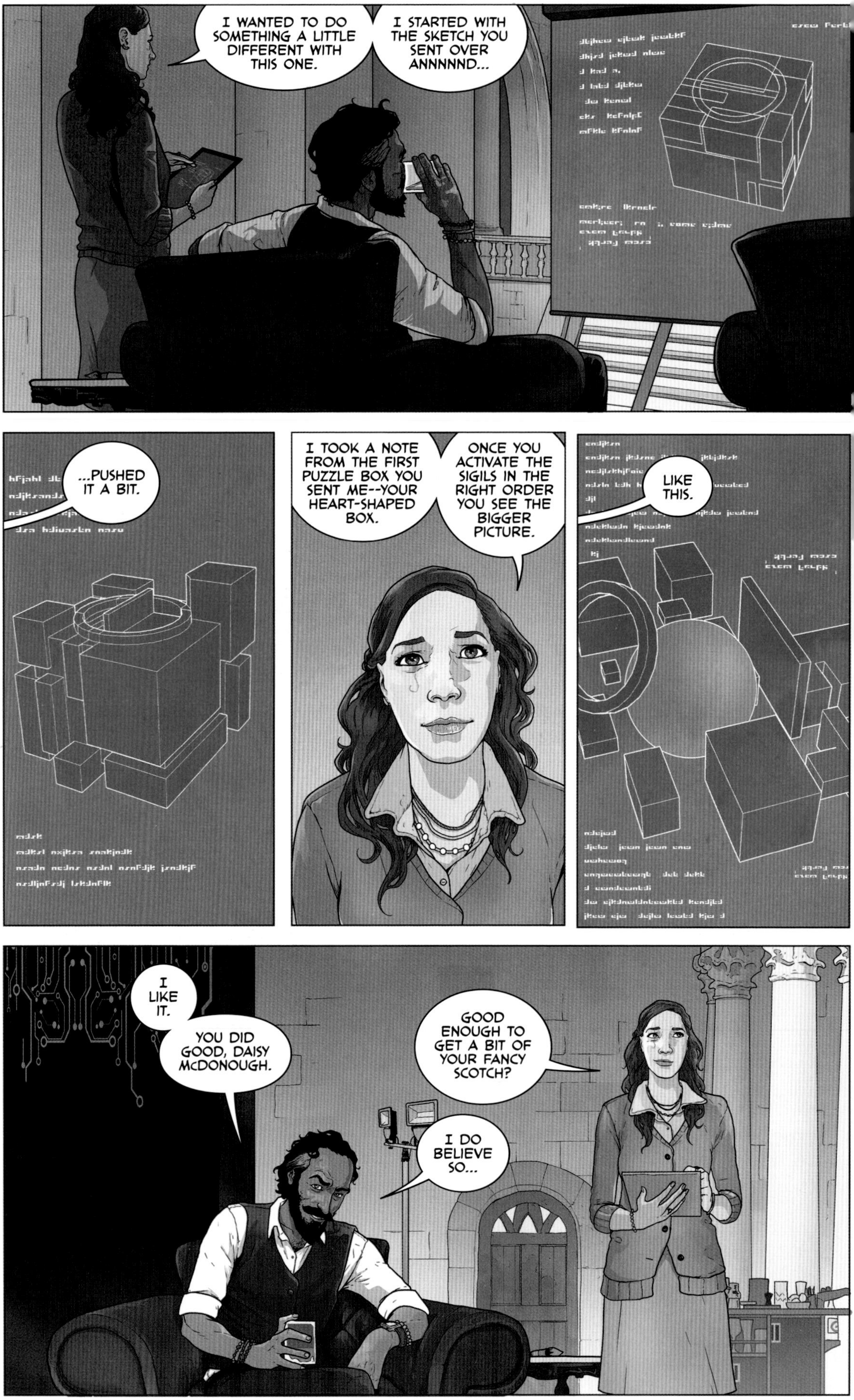
I WANTED TO DO SOMETHING A LITTLE DIFFERENT WITH THIS ONE.
I STARTED WITH THE SKETCH YOU SENT OVER ANNNNND...
...PUSHED IT A BIT.
I TOOK A NOTE FROM THE FIRST PUZZLE BOX YOU SENT ME--YOUR HEART-SHAPED BOX.
ONCE YOU ACTIVATE THE SIGILS IN THE RIGHT ORDER YOU SEE THE BIGGER PICTURE.
LIKE THIS.
I LIKE IT.
YOU DID GOOD, DAISY McDONOUGH.
GOOD ENOUGH TO GET A BIT OF YOUR FANCY SCOTCH?
I DO BELIEVE SO...

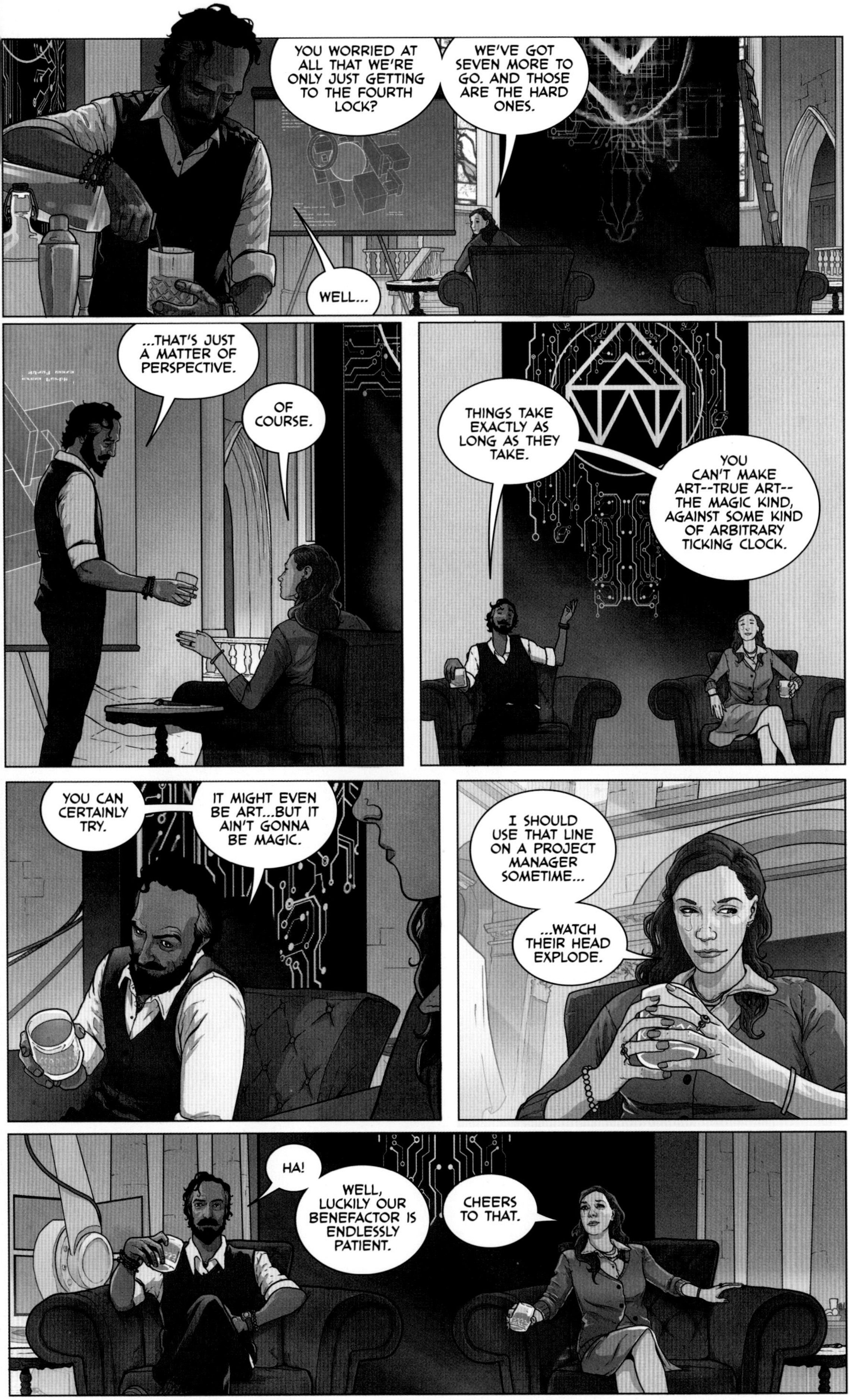
YOU WORRIED AT ALL THAT WE'RE ONLY JUST GETTING TO THE FOURTH LOCK?
WE'VE GOT SEVEN MORE TO GO. AND THOSE ARE THE HARD ONES.
WELL...
...THAT'S JUST A MATTER OF PERSPECTIVE.
OF COURSE.
THINGS TAKE EXACTLY AS LONG AS THEY TAKE.
YOU CAN'T MAKE ART--TRUE ART--THE MAGIC KIND, AGAINST SOME KIND OF ARBITRARY TICKING CLOCK.
YOU CAN CERTAINLY TRY.
IT MIGHT EVEN BE ART...BUT IT AIN'T GONNA BE MAGIC.
I SHOULD USE THAT LINE ON A PROJECT MANAGER SOMETIME...
...WATCH THEIR HEAD EXPLODE.
HA!
WELL, LUCKILY OUR BENEFACTOR IS ENDLESSLY PATIENT.
CHEERS TO THAT.

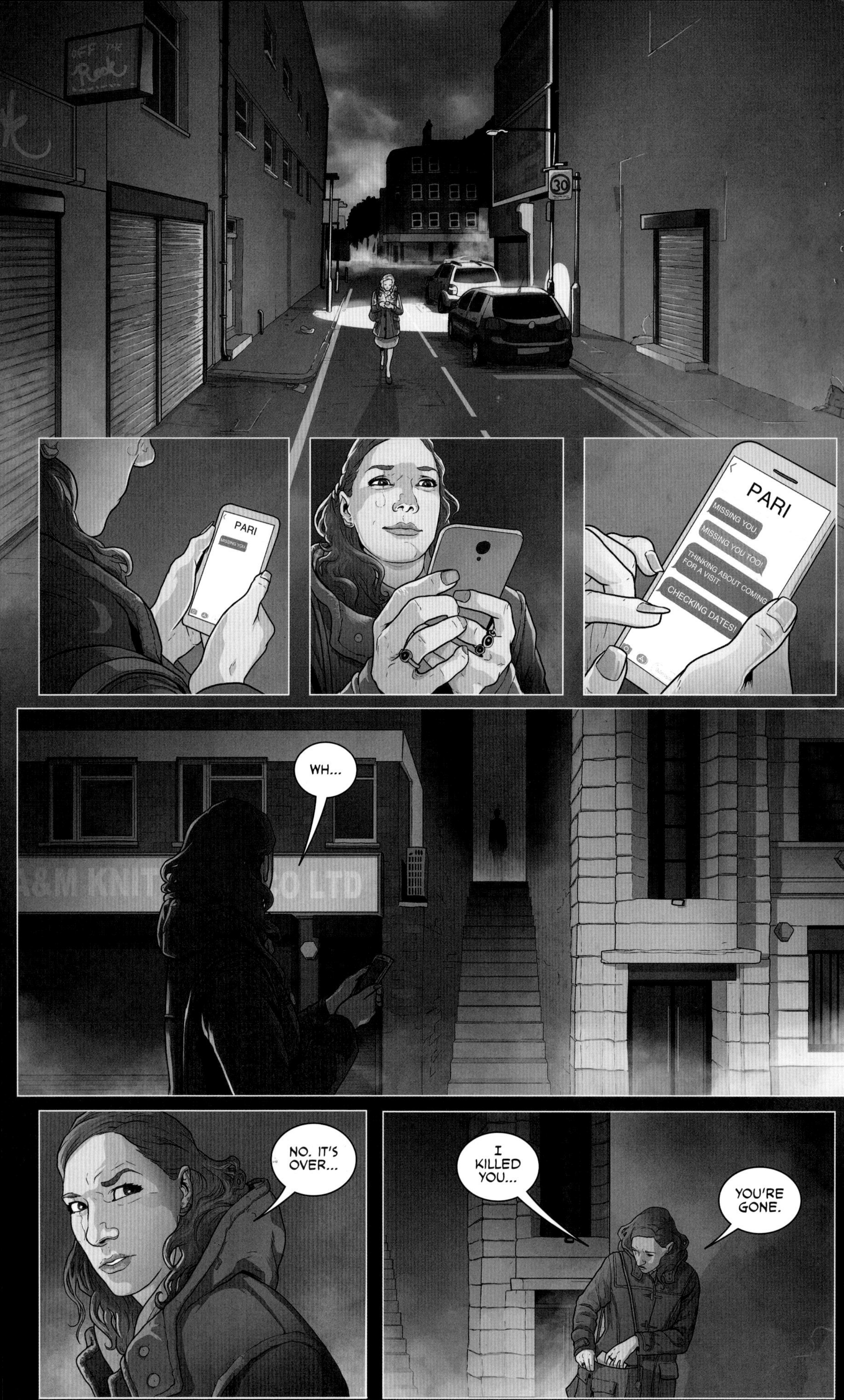
30
PARI
MISSING YOU.
PARI
MISSING YOU.
MISSING YOU TOO!
THINKING ABOUT COMING FOR A VISIT.
CHECKING DATES!
WH...
NO. IT'S OVER...
I KILLED YOU...
YOU'RE GONE.

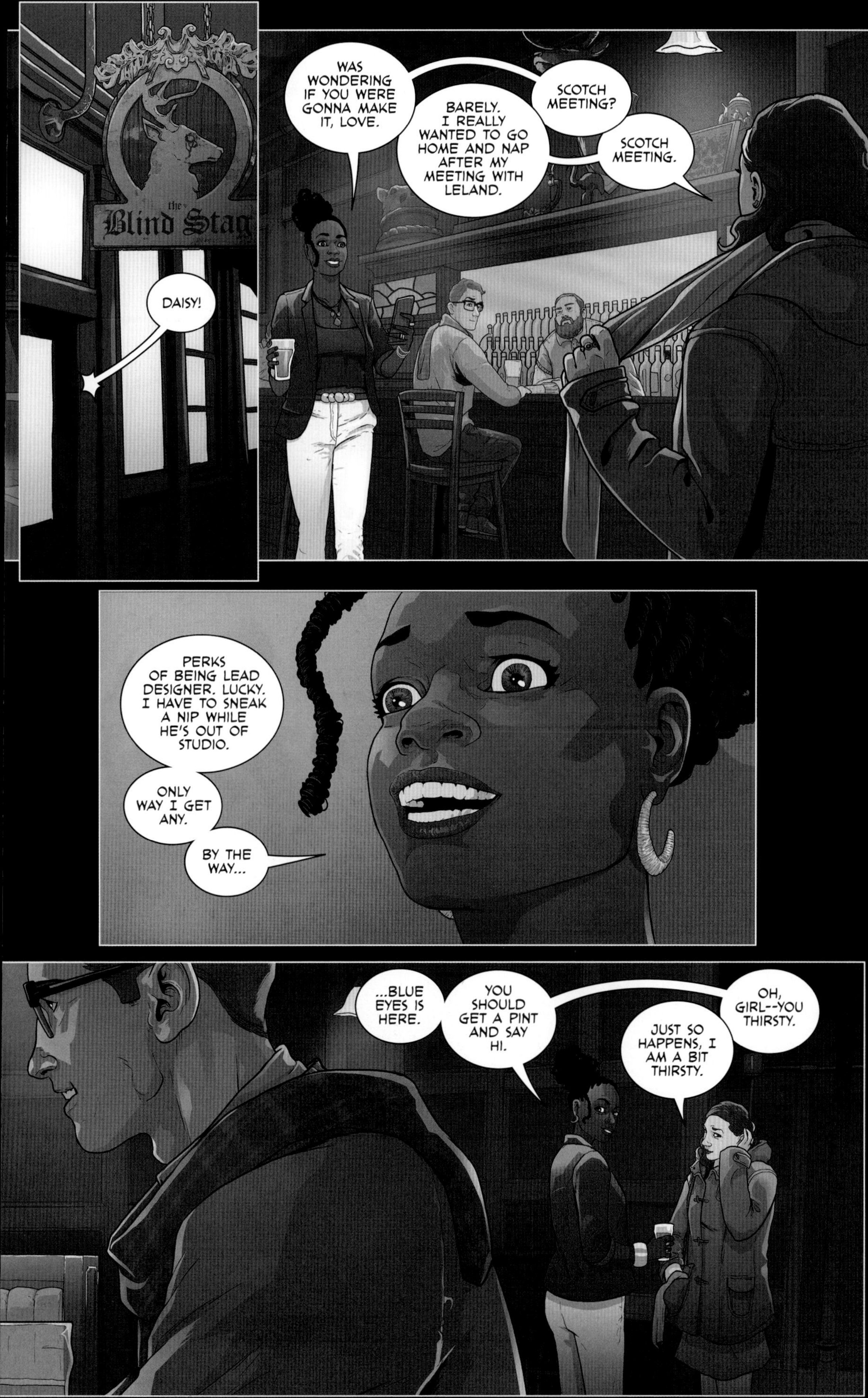
the Blind Stag
DAISY!
WAS WONDERING IF YOU WERE GONNA MAKE IT, LOVE.
BARELY. I REALLY WANTED TO GO HOME AND NAP AFTER MY MEETING WITH LELAND.
SCOTCH MEETING?
SCOTCH MEETING.
PERKS OF BEING LEAD DESIGNER. LUCKY. I HAVE TO SNEAK A NIP WHILE HE'S OUT OF STUDIO.
ONLY WAY I GET ANY.
BY THE WAY...
...BLUE EYES IS HERE.
YOU SHOULD GET A PINT AND SAY HI.
JUST SO HAPPENS, I AM A BIT THIRSTY.
OH, GIRL--YOU THIRSTY.

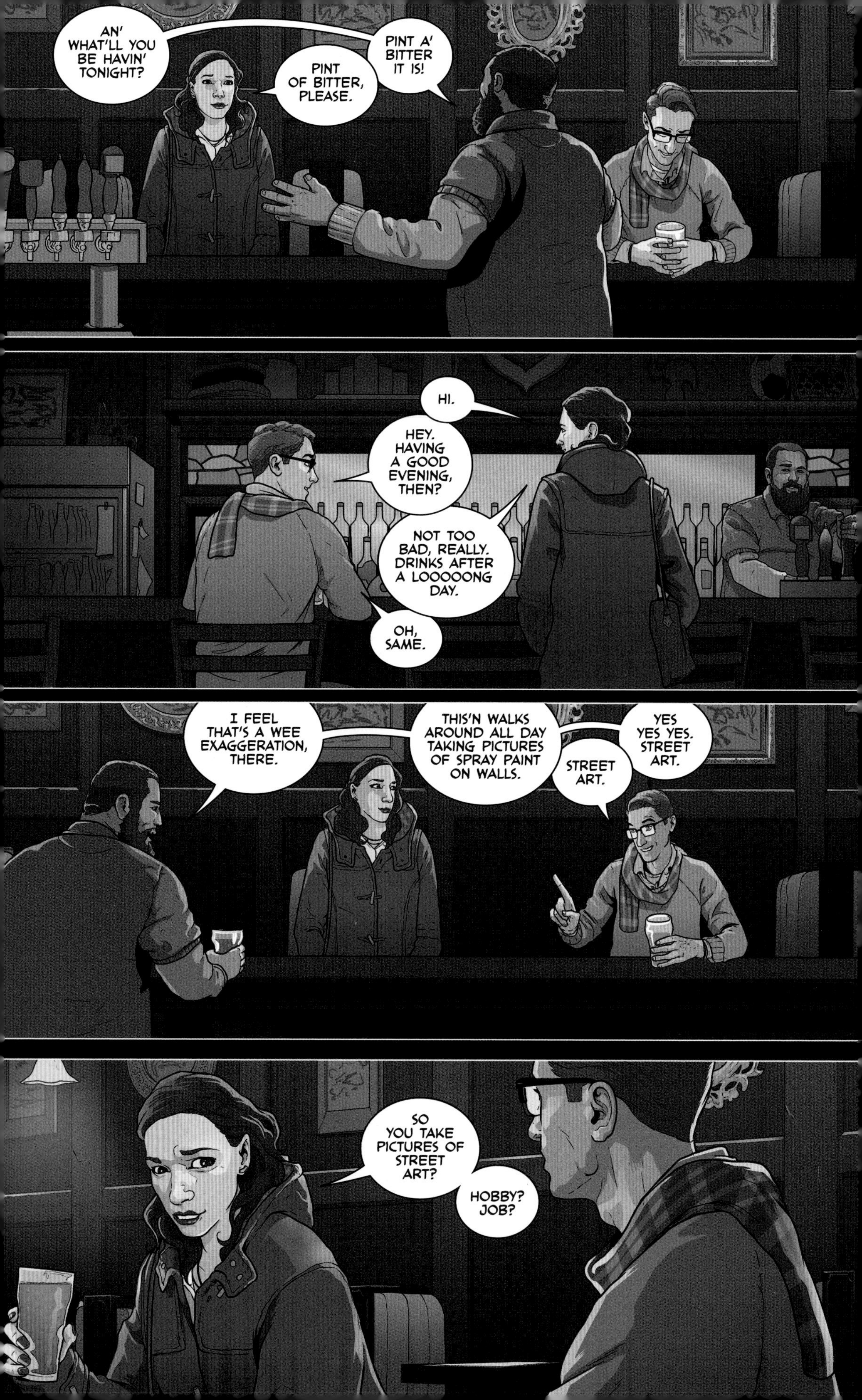
AN' WHAT'LL YOU BE HAVIN' TONIGHT?
PINT OF BITTER, PLEASE.
PINT A' BITTER IT IS!
HI.
HEY. HAVING A GOOD EVENING, THEN?
NOT TOO BAD, REALLY. DRINKS AFTER A LOOOOONG DAY.
OH, SAME.
THIS'N WALKS AROUND ALL DAY TAKING PICTURES OF SPRAY PAINT ON WALLS.
STREET ART.
YES YES YES. STREET ART.
I FEEL THAT'S A WEE EXAGGERATION, THERE.
SO YOU TAKE PICTURES OF STREET ART?
HOBBY? JOB?

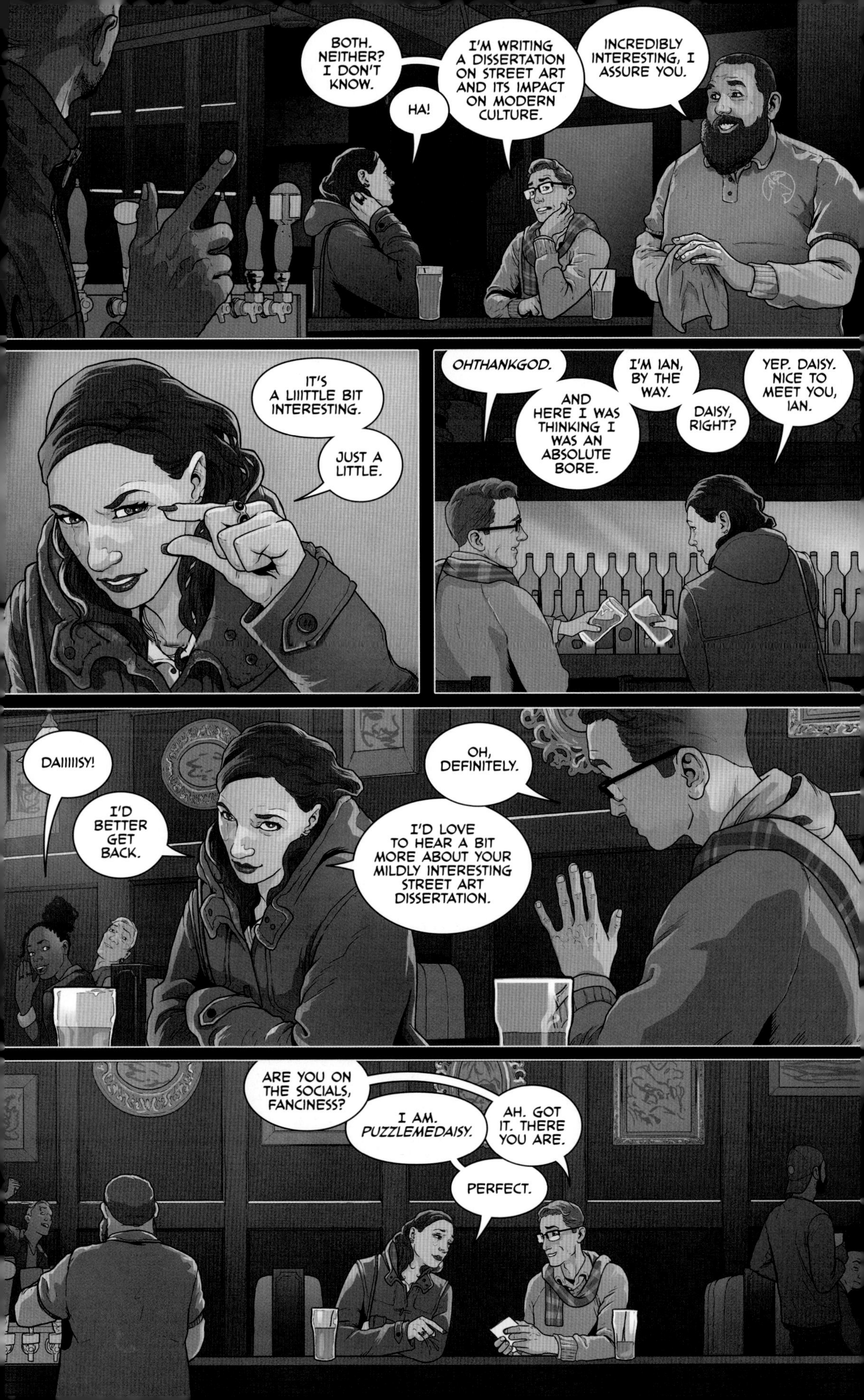
BOTH. NEITHER? I DON'T KNOW.
HA!
I'M WRITING A DISSERTATION ON STREET ART AND ITS IMPACT ON MODERN CULTURE.
INCREDIBLY INTERESTING, I ASSURE YOU.
IT'S A LIIITTLE BIT INTERESTING.
JUST A LITTLE.
OHTHANKGOD.
AND HERE I WAS THINKING I WAS AN ABSOLUTE BORE.
I'M IAN, BY THE WAY.
DAISY, RIGHT?
YEP. DAISY. NICE TO MEET YOU, IAN.
DAIIIIISY!
I'D BETTER GET BACK.
I'D LOVE TO HEAR A BIT MORE ABOUT YOUR MILDLY INTERESTING STREET ART DISSERTATION.
OH, DEFINITELY.
ARE YOU ON THE SOCIALS, FANCINESS?
I AM. PUZZLEMEDAISY.
AH. GOT IT. THERE YOU ARE.
PERFECT.

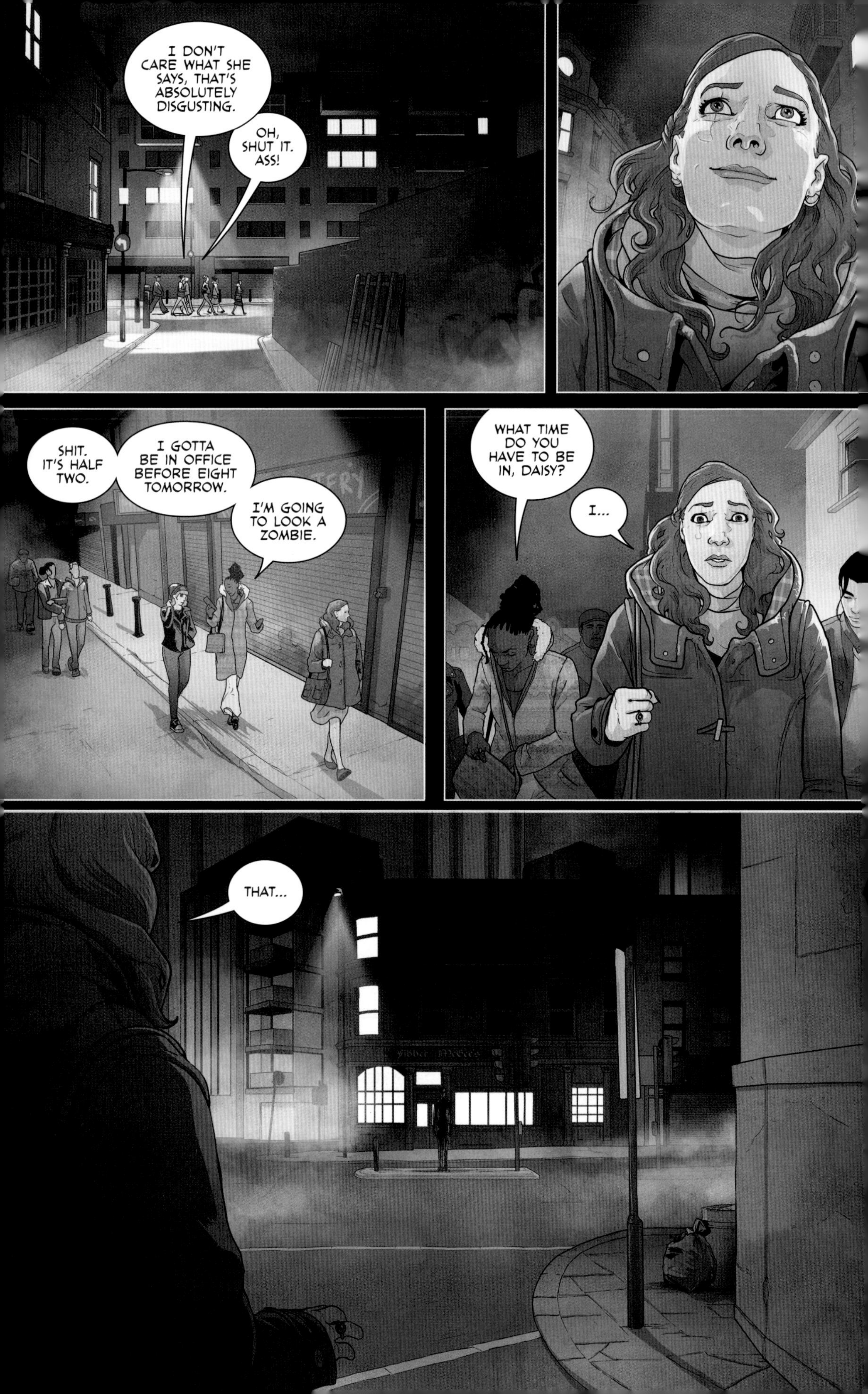
I DON'T CARE WHAT SHE SAYS, THAT'S ABSOLUTELY DISGUSTING.
OH, SHUT IT. ASS!
SHIT. IT'S HALF TWO.
I GOTTA BE IN OFFICE BEFORE EIGHT TOMORROW.
I'M GOING TO LOOK A ZOMBIE.
WHAT TIME DO YOU HAVE TO BE IN, DAISY?
I...
THAT...

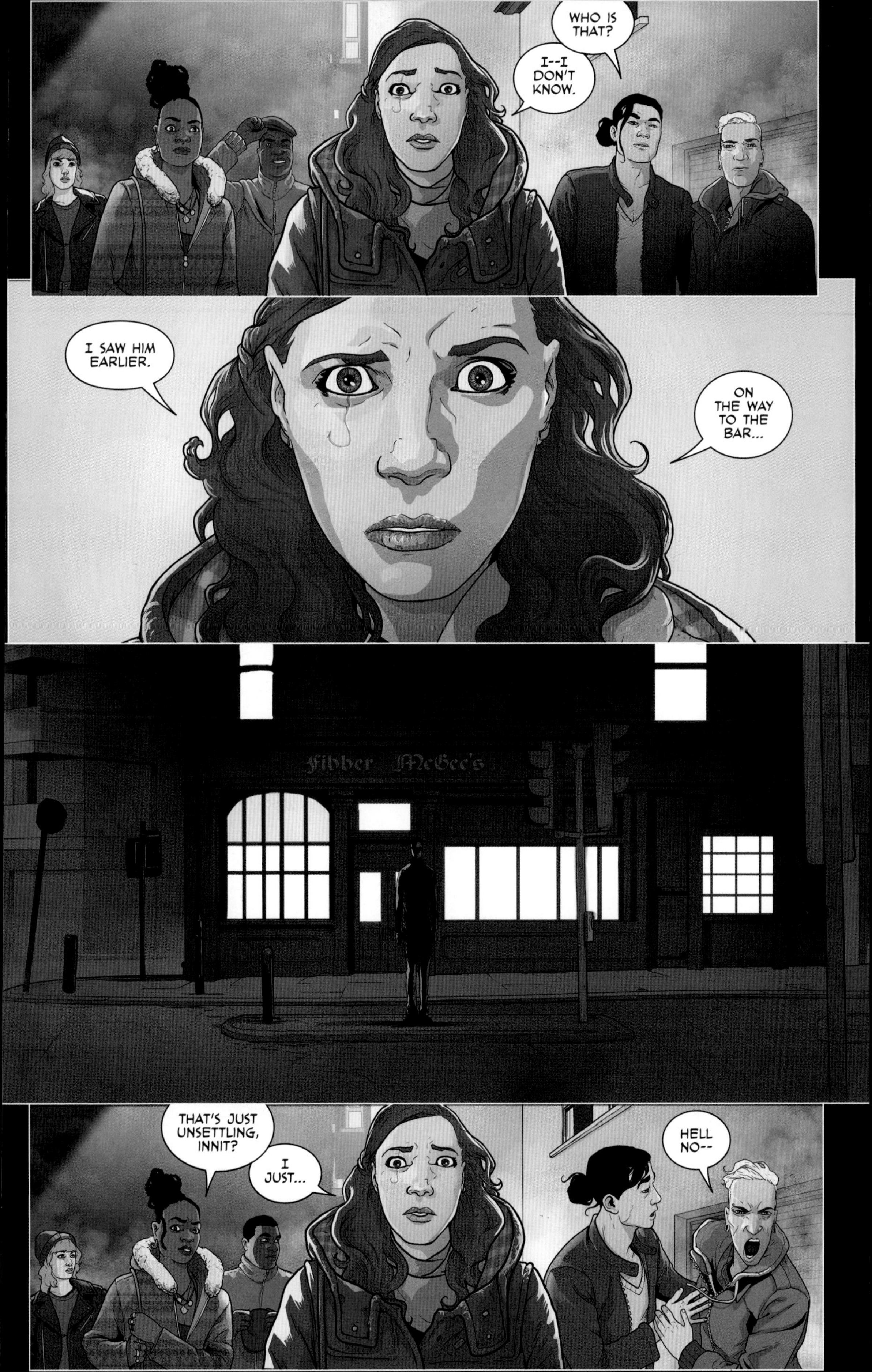
WHO IS THAT?
I--I DON'T KNOW.
I SAW HIM EARLIER.
ON THE WAY TO THE BAR...
Fibber McGee's
THAT'S JUST UNSETTLING, INNIT?
I JUST...
HELL NO--

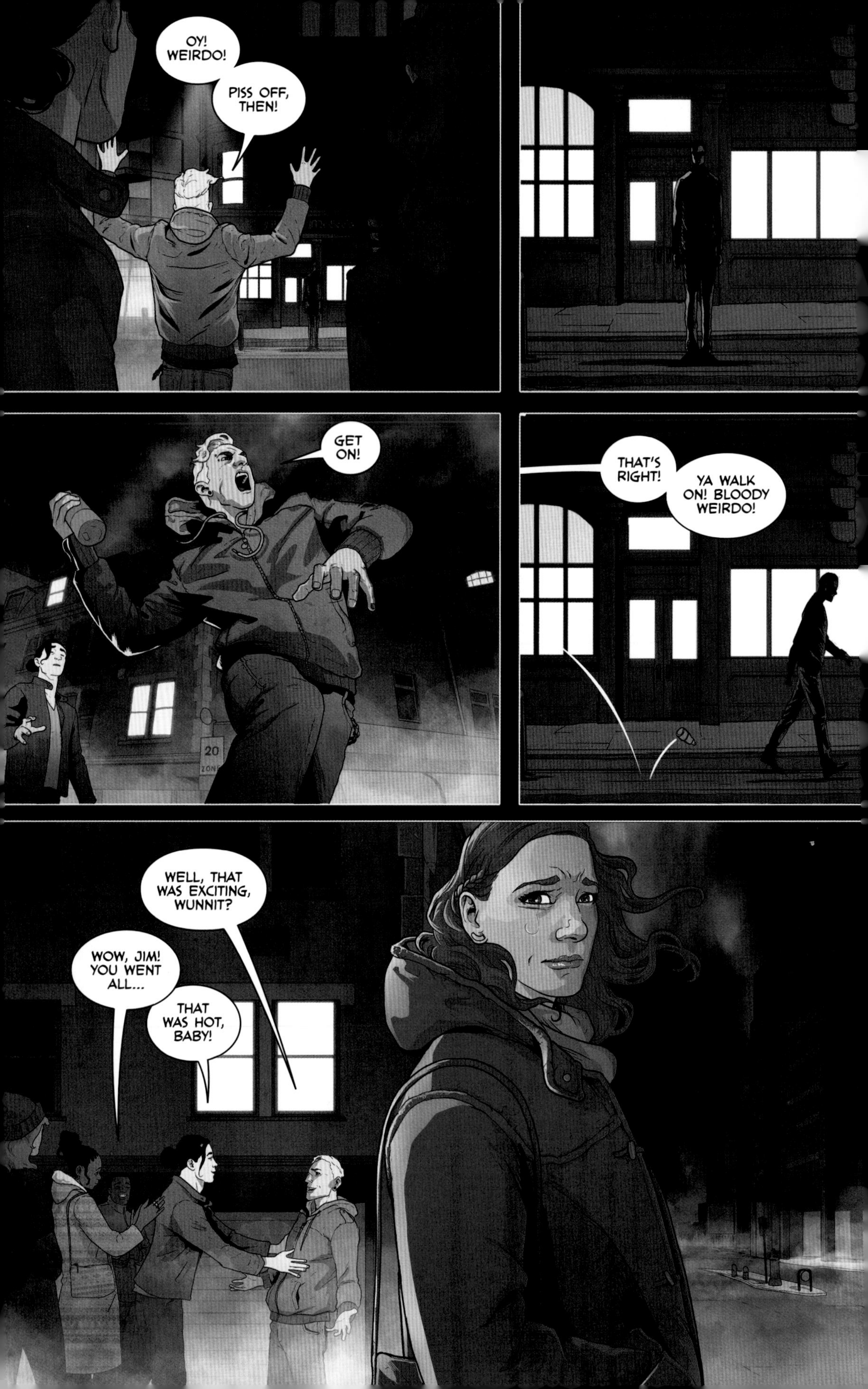
OY! WEIRDO!
PISS OFF, THEN!
GET ON!
THAT'S RIGHT!
YA WALK ON! BLOODY WEIRDO!
WELL, THAT WAS EXCITING, WUNNIT?
WOW, JIM! YOU WENT ALL...
THAT WAS HOT, BABY!
20
ZONE

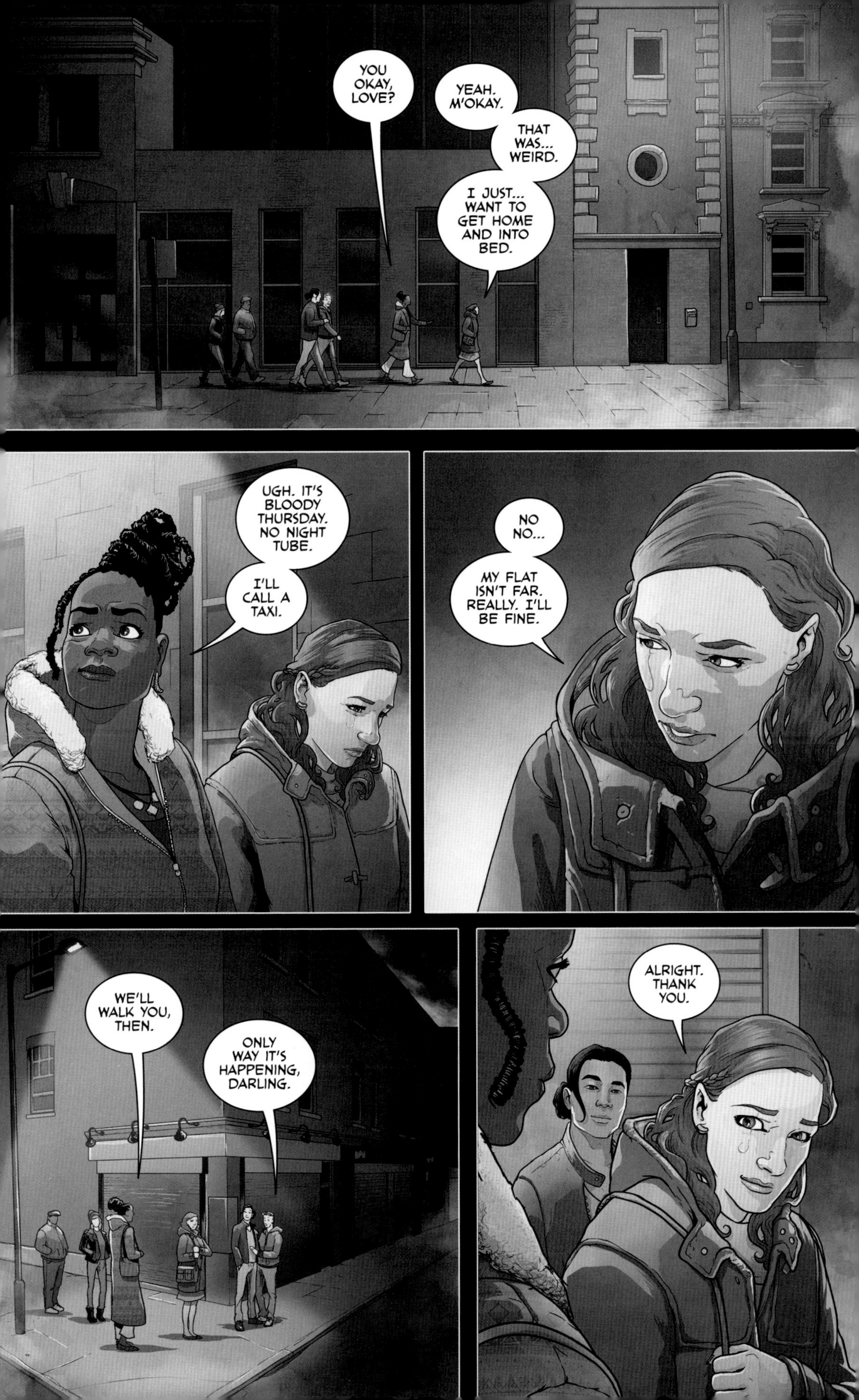
YOU OKAY, LOVE?
YEAH. M'OKAY.
THAT WAS... WEIRD.
I JUST... WANT TO GET HOME AND INTO BED.
UGH. IT'S BLOODY THURSDAY. NO NIGHT TUBE.
I'LL CALL A TAXI.
NO NO...
MY FLAT ISN'T FAR. REALLY. I'LL BE FINE.
WE'LL WALK YOU, THEN.
ONLY WAY IT'S HAPPENING, DARLING.
ALRIGHT. THANK YOU.

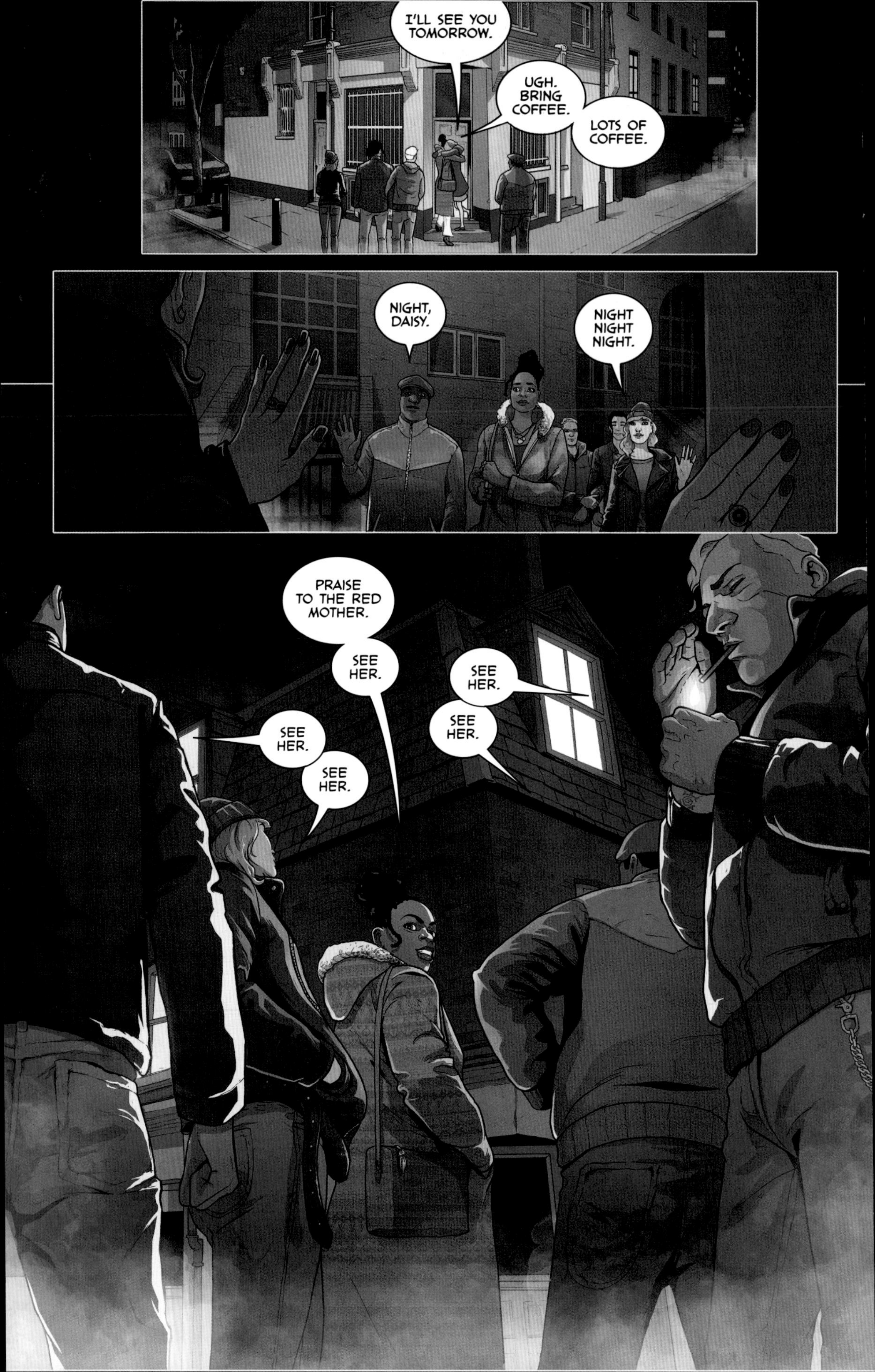
I'LL SEE YOU TOMORROW.
UGH. BRING COFFEE.
LOTS OF COFFEE.
NIGHT, DAISY.
NIGHT NIGHT NIGHT.
PRAISE TO THE RED MOTHER.
SEE HER.
SEE HER.
SEE HER.
SEE HER.
SEE HER.
SEE HER.

CHAPTER
SEVEN

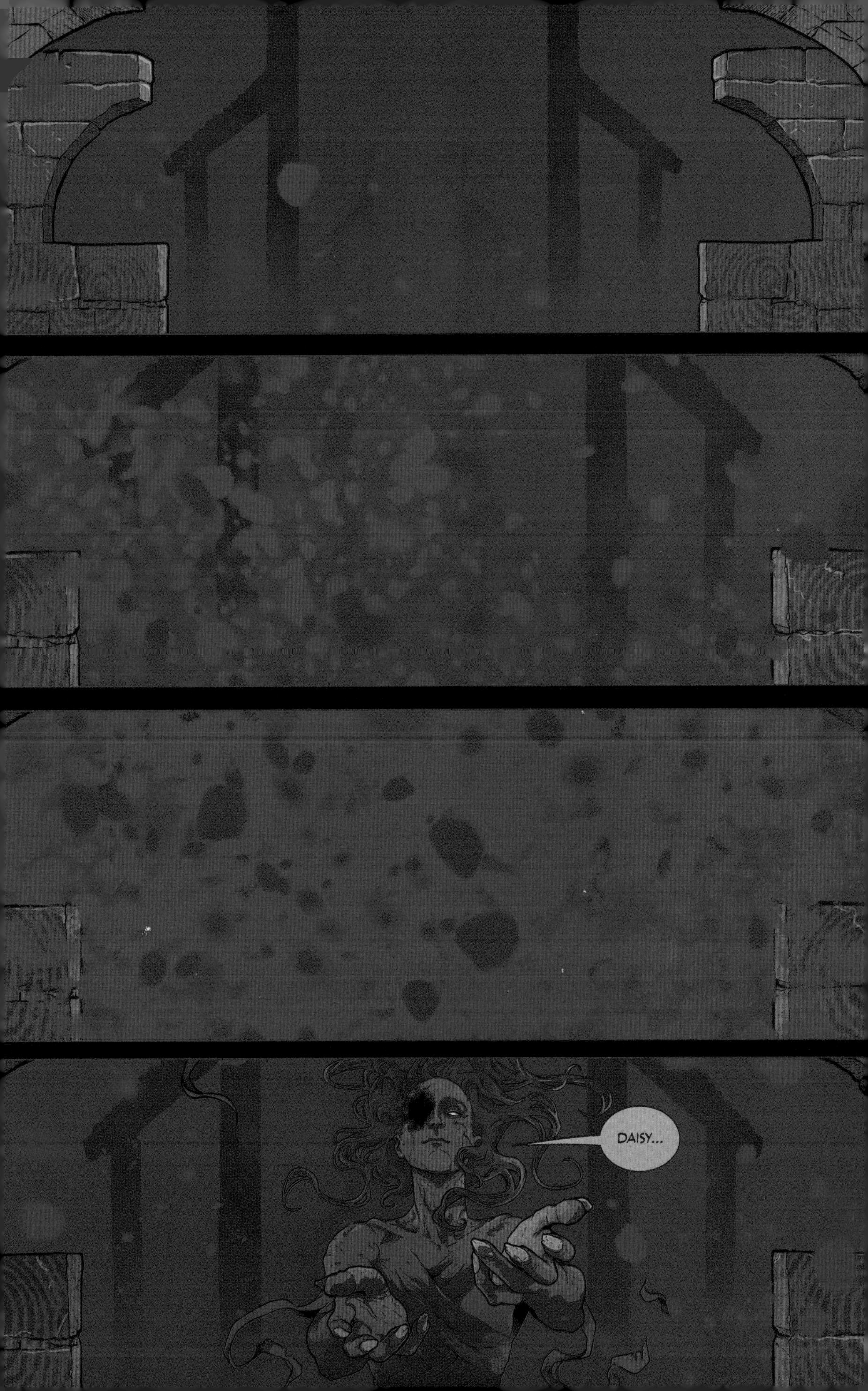
DAISY...

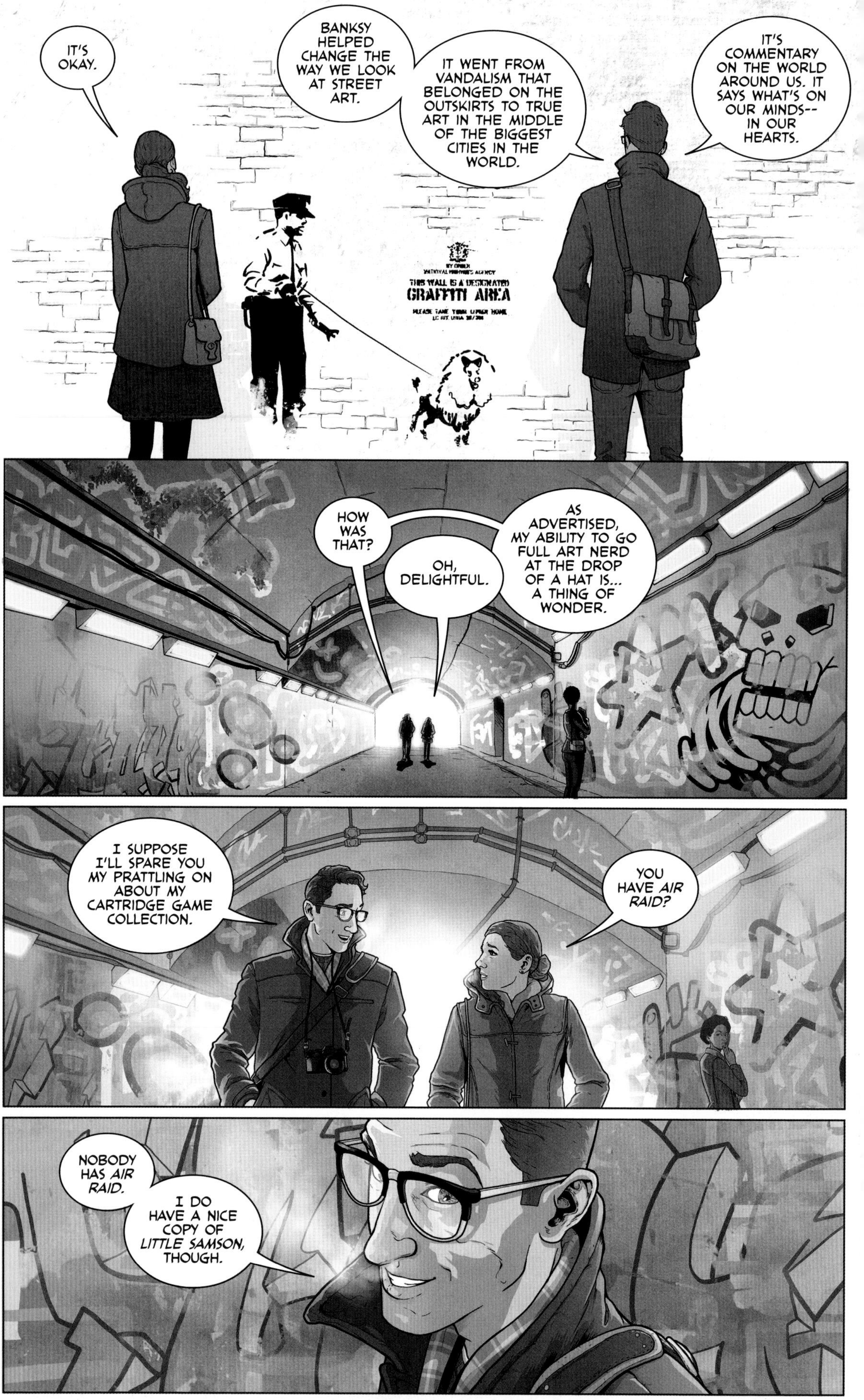
IT'S OKAY.
BANKSY HELPED CHANGE THE WAY WE LOOK AT STREET ART.
IT WENT FROM VANDALISM THAT BELONGED ON THE OUTSKIRTS TO TRUE ART IN THE MIDDLE OF THE BIGGEST CITIES IN THE WORLD.
THIS WALL IS A DESIGNATED
GRAFFITI AREA
IT'S COMMENTARY ON THE WORLD AROUND US. IT SAYS WHAT'S ON OUR MINDS-- IN OUR HEARTS.
HOW WAS THAT?
OH, DELIGHTFUL.
AS ADVERTISED, MY ABILITY TO GO FULL ART NERD AT THE DROP OF A HAT IS... A THING OF WONDER.
I SUPPOSE I'LL SPARE YOU MY PRATTLING ON ABOUT MY CARTRIDGE GAME COLLECTION.
YOU HAVE *AIR RAID?*
NOBODY HAS *AIR RAID.*
I DO HAVE A NICE COPY OF *LITTLE SAMSON,* THOUGH.

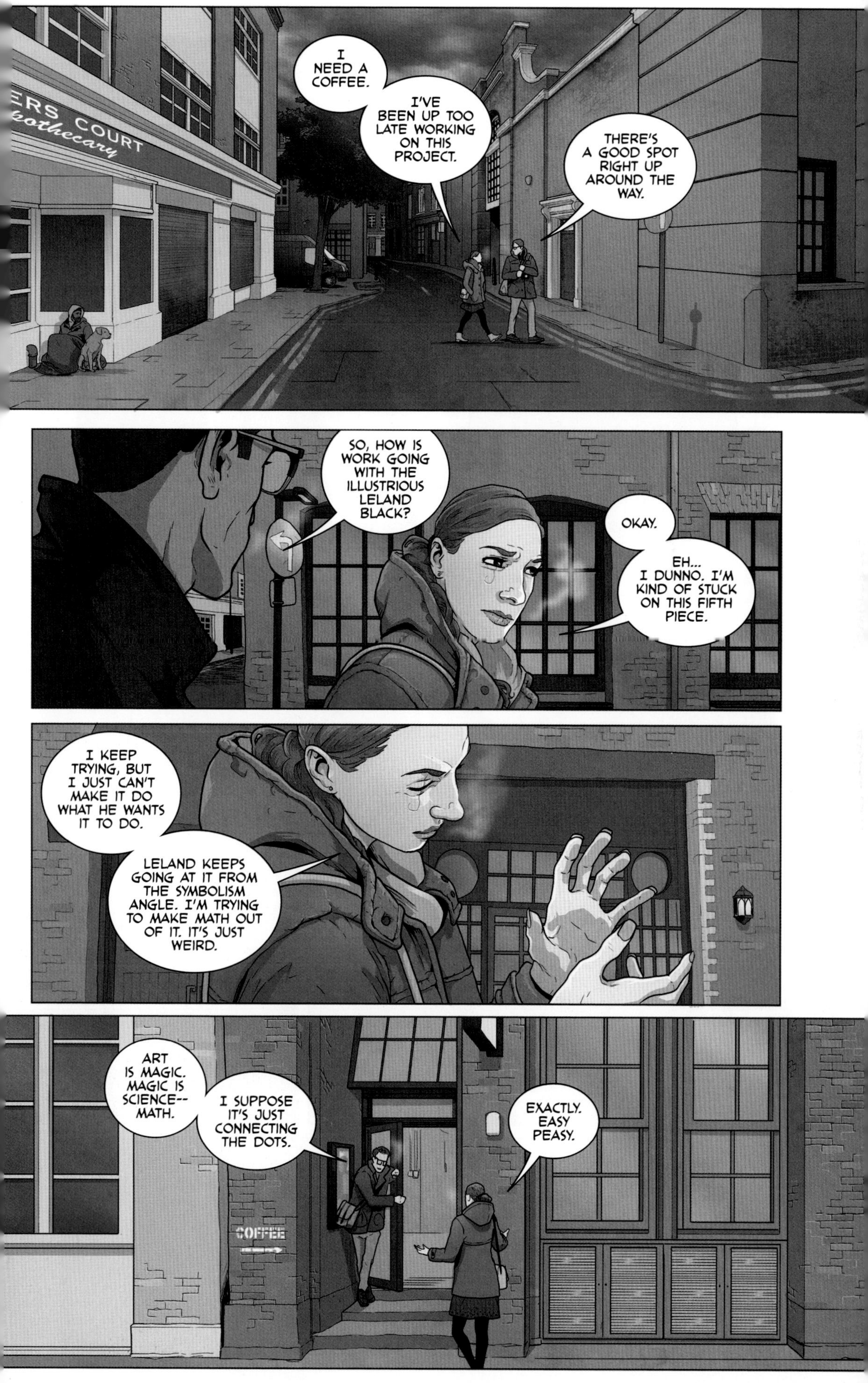
ERS COURT
pothecary
I NEED A COFFEE.
I'VE BEEN UP TOO LATE WORKING ON THIS PROJECT.
THERE'S A GOOD SPOT RIGHT UP AROUND THE WAY.
SO, HOW IS WORK GOING WITH THE ILLUSTRIOUS LELAND BLACK?
OKAY.
EH... I DUNNO. I'M KIND OF STUCK ON THIS FIFTH PIECE.
I KEEP TRYING, BUT I JUST CAN'T MAKE IT DO WHAT HE WANTS IT TO DO.
LELAND KEEPS GOING AT IT FROM THE SYMBOLISM ANGLE. I'M TRYING TO MAKE MATH OUT OF IT. IT'S JUST WEIRD.
ART IS MAGIC. MAGIC IS SCIENCE-- MATH.
I SUPPOSE IT'S JUST CONNECTING THE DOTS.
EXACTLY. EASY PEASY.
COFFEE

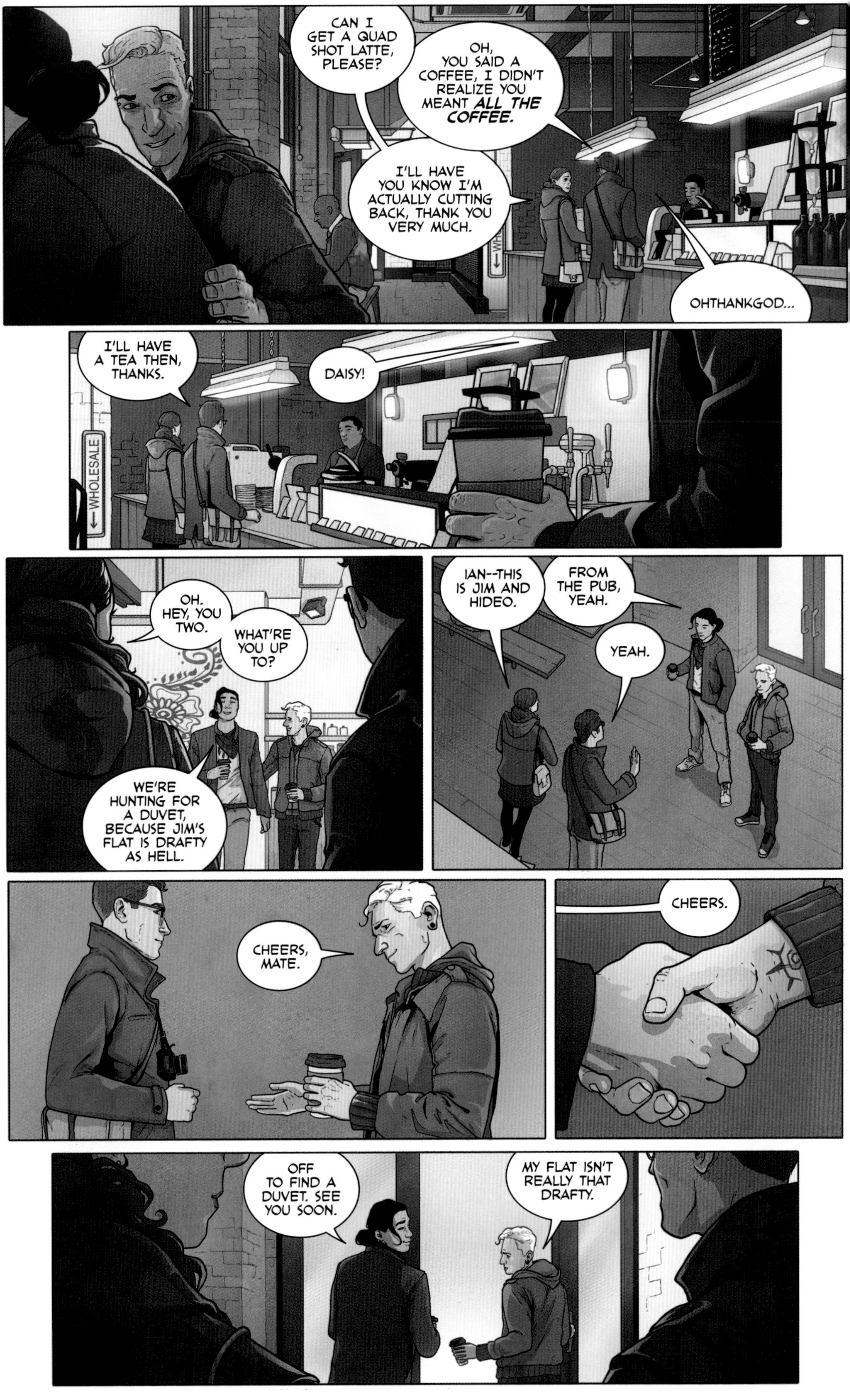
CAN I GET A QUAD SHOT LATTE, PLEASE?
OH, YOU SAID A COFFEE, I DIDN'T REALIZE YOU MEANT ALL THE COFFEE.
I'LL HAVE YOU KNOW I'M ACTUALLY CUTTING BACK, THANK YOU VERY MUCH.
OHTHANKGOD...
I'LL HAVE A TEA THEN, THANKS.
DAISY!
WHOLESALE
OH. HEY, YOU TWO.
WHAT'RE YOU UP TO?
WE'RE HUNTING FOR A DUVET, BECAUSE JIM'S FLAT IS DRAFTY AS HELL.
IAN--THIS IS JIM AND HIDEO.
FROM THE PUB, YEAH.
YEAH.
CHEERS, MATE.
CHEERS.
OFF TO FIND A DUVET. SEE YOU SOON.
MY FLAT ISN'T REALLY THAT DRAFTY.

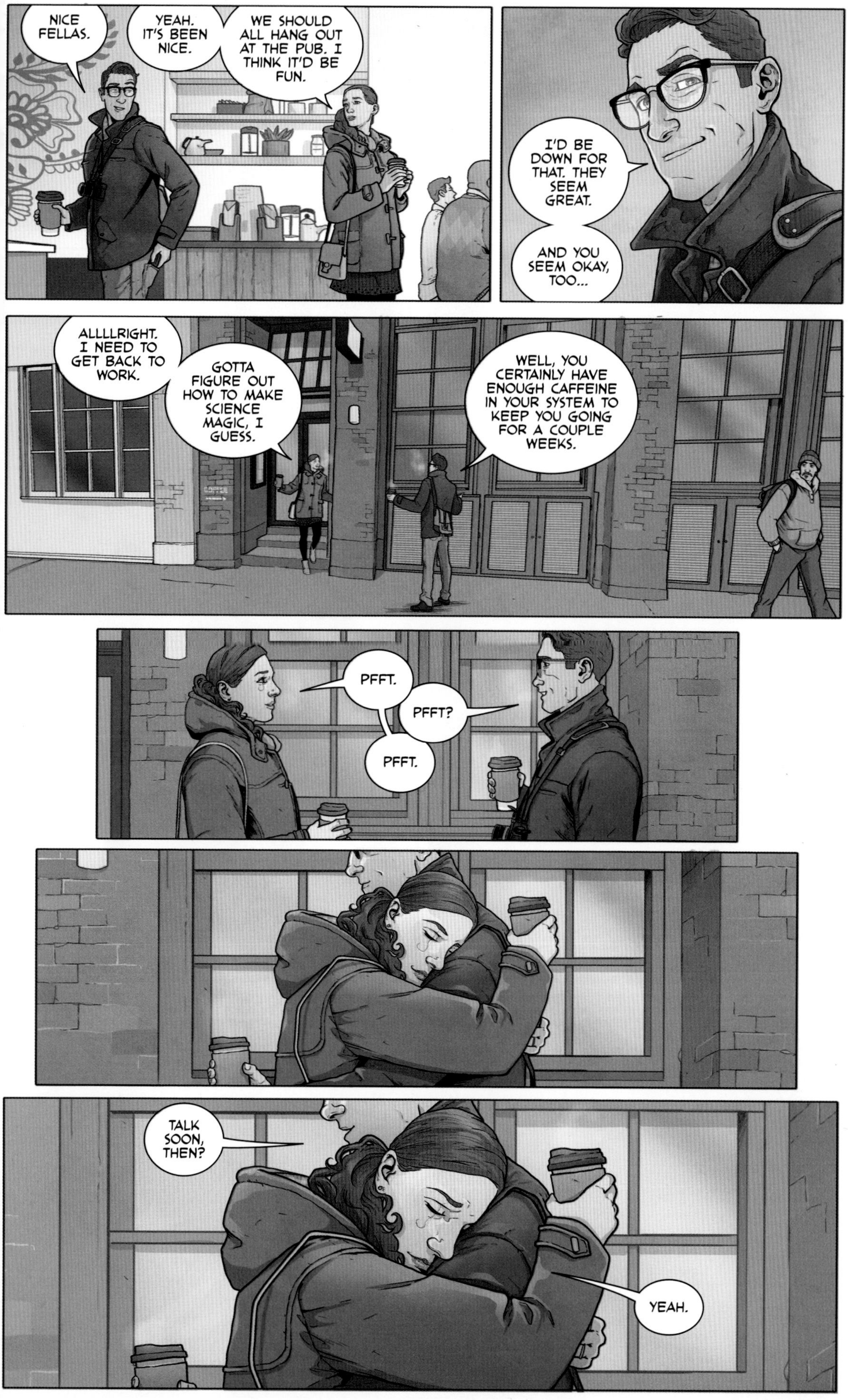
NICE FELLAS.
YEAH. IT'S BEEN NICE.
WE SHOULD ALL HANG OUT AT THE PUB. I THINK IT'D BE FUN.
I'D BE DOWN FOR THAT. THEY SEEM GREAT.
AND YOU SEEM OKAY, TOO...
ALLLLRIGHT. I NEED TO GET BACK TO WORK.
GOTTA FIGURE OUT HOW TO MAKE SCIENCE MAGIC, I GUESS.
WELL, YOU CERTAINLY HAVE ENOUGH CAFFEINE IN YOUR SYSTEM TO KEEP YOU GOING FOR A COUPLE WEEKS.
PFFT.
PFFT?
PFFT.
TALK SOON, THEN?
YEAH.

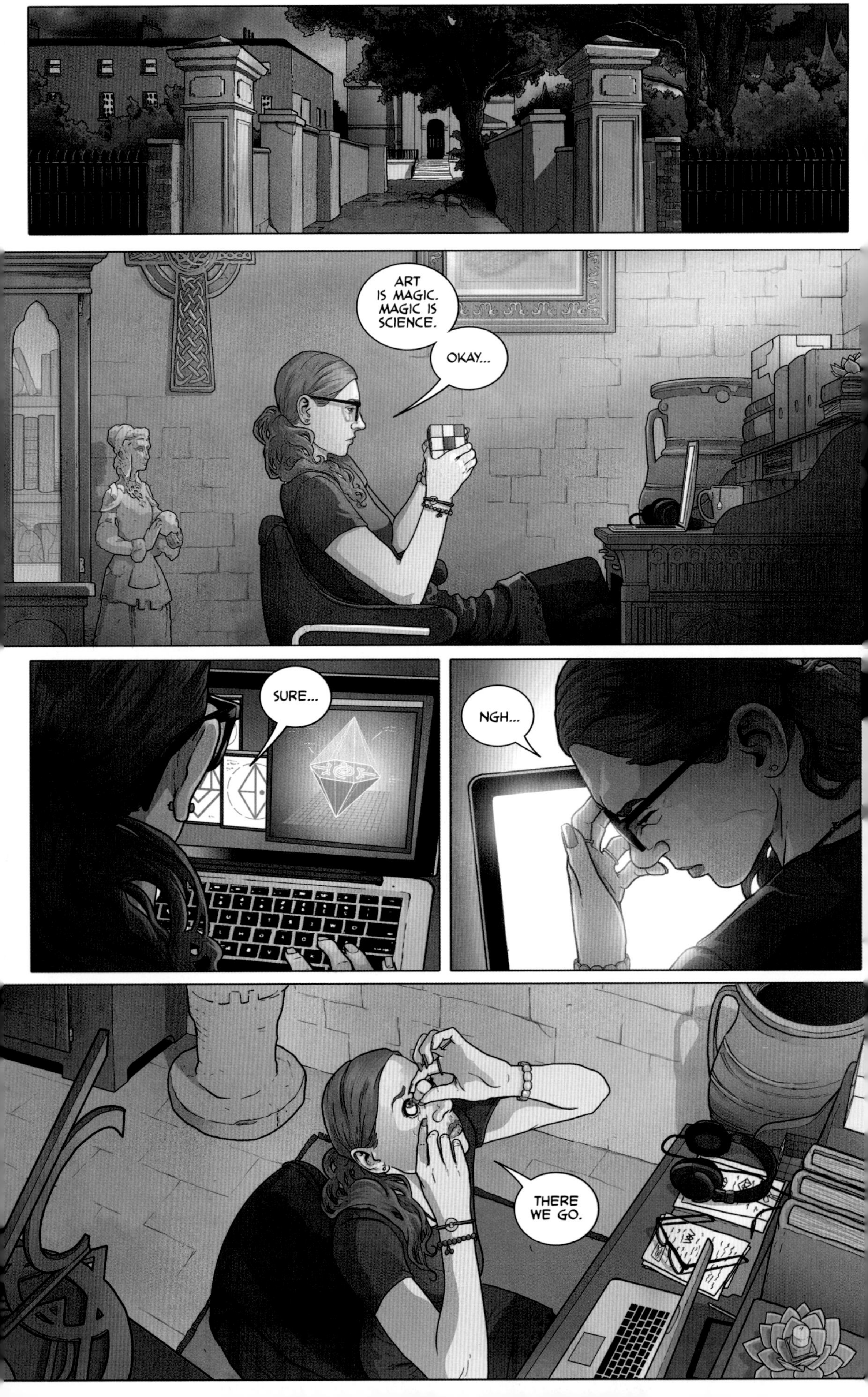
ART IS MAGIC. MAGIC IS SCIENCE.
OKAY...
SURE...
NGH...
THERE WE GO.

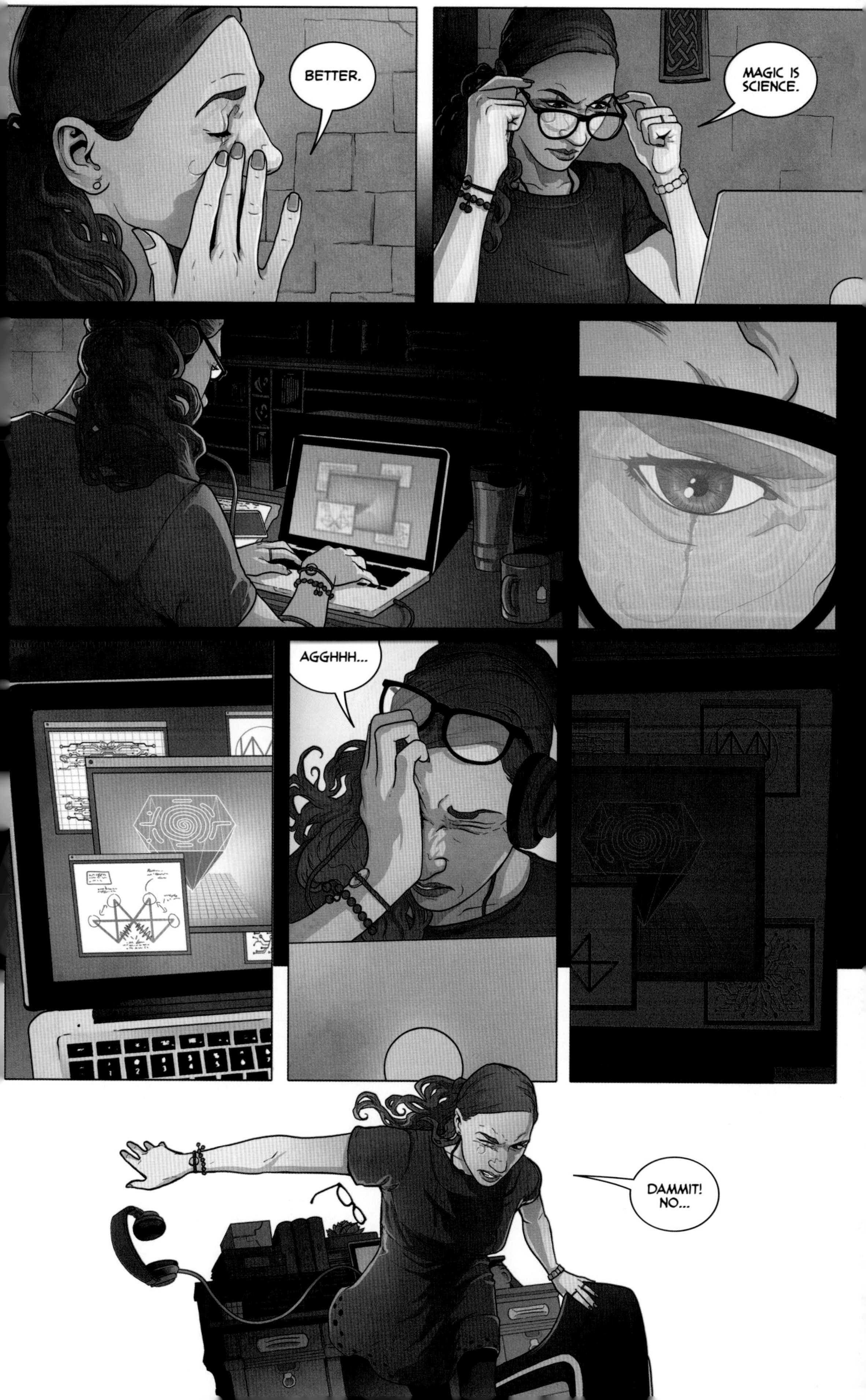
BETTER.
MAGIC IS SCIENCE.
AGGHHH...
DAMMIT! NO...

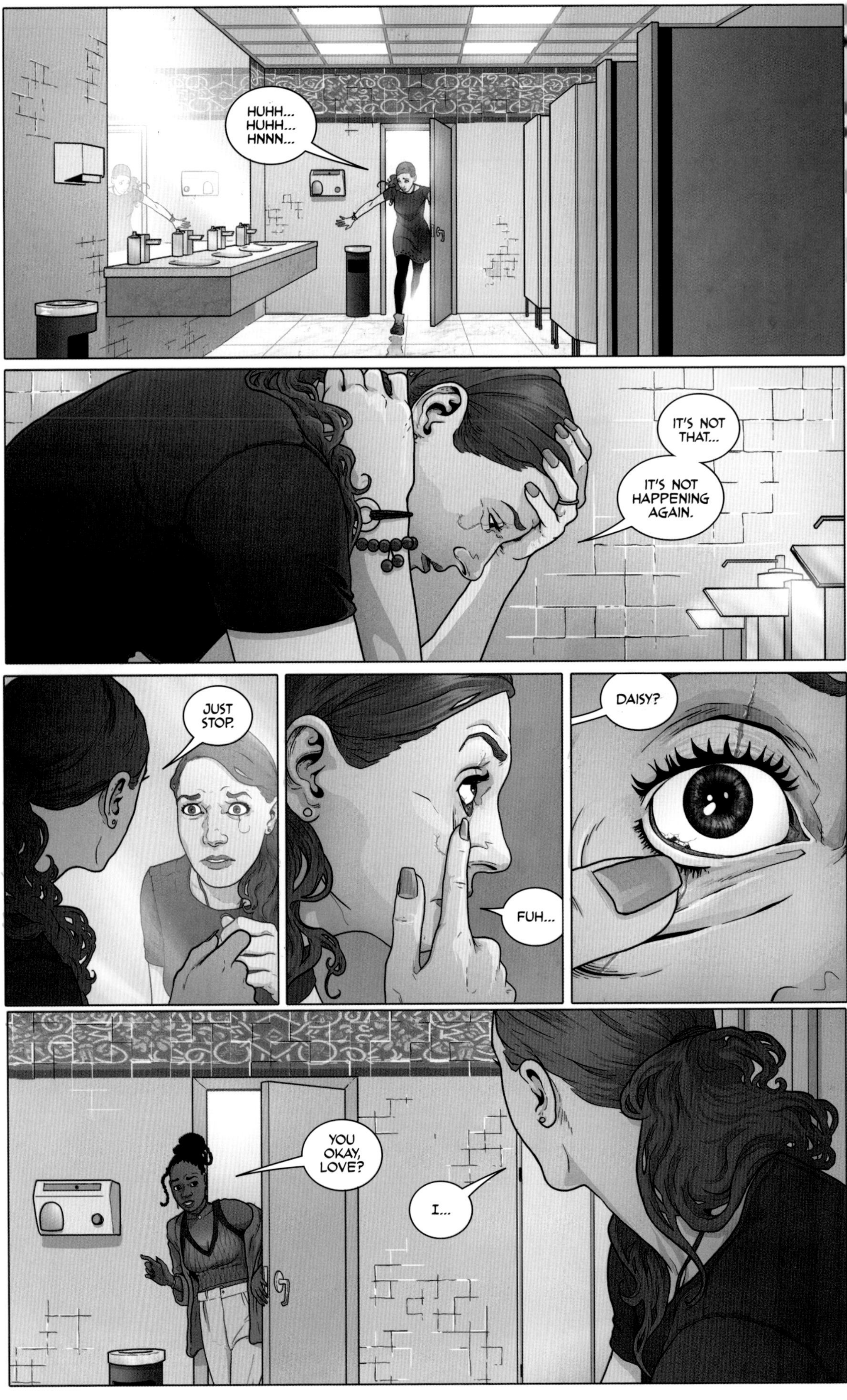
HUHH...
HUHH...
HNNN...
IT'S NOT THAT...
IT'S NOT HAPPENING AGAIN.
JUST STOP.
FUH...
DAISY?
YOU OKAY, LOVE?
I...

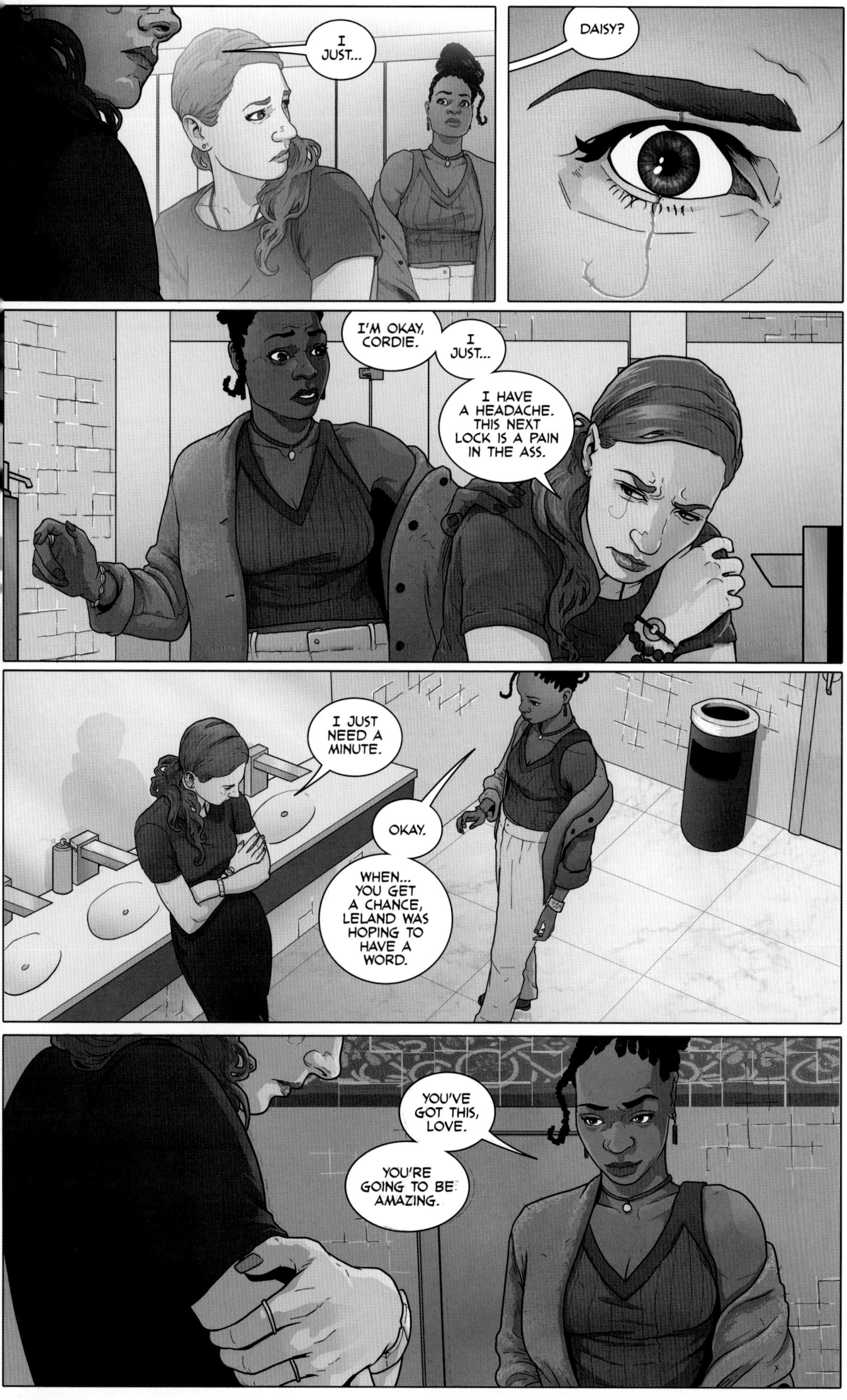
I JUST...
DAISY?
I'M OKAY, CORDIE.
I JUST...
I HAVE A HEADACHE. THIS NEXT LOCK IS A PAIN IN THE ASS.
I JUST NEED A MINUTE.
OKAY.
WHEN... YOU GET A CHANCE, LELAND WAS HOPING TO HAVE A WORD.
YOU'VE GOT THIS, LOVE.
YOU'RE GOING TO BE AMAZING.

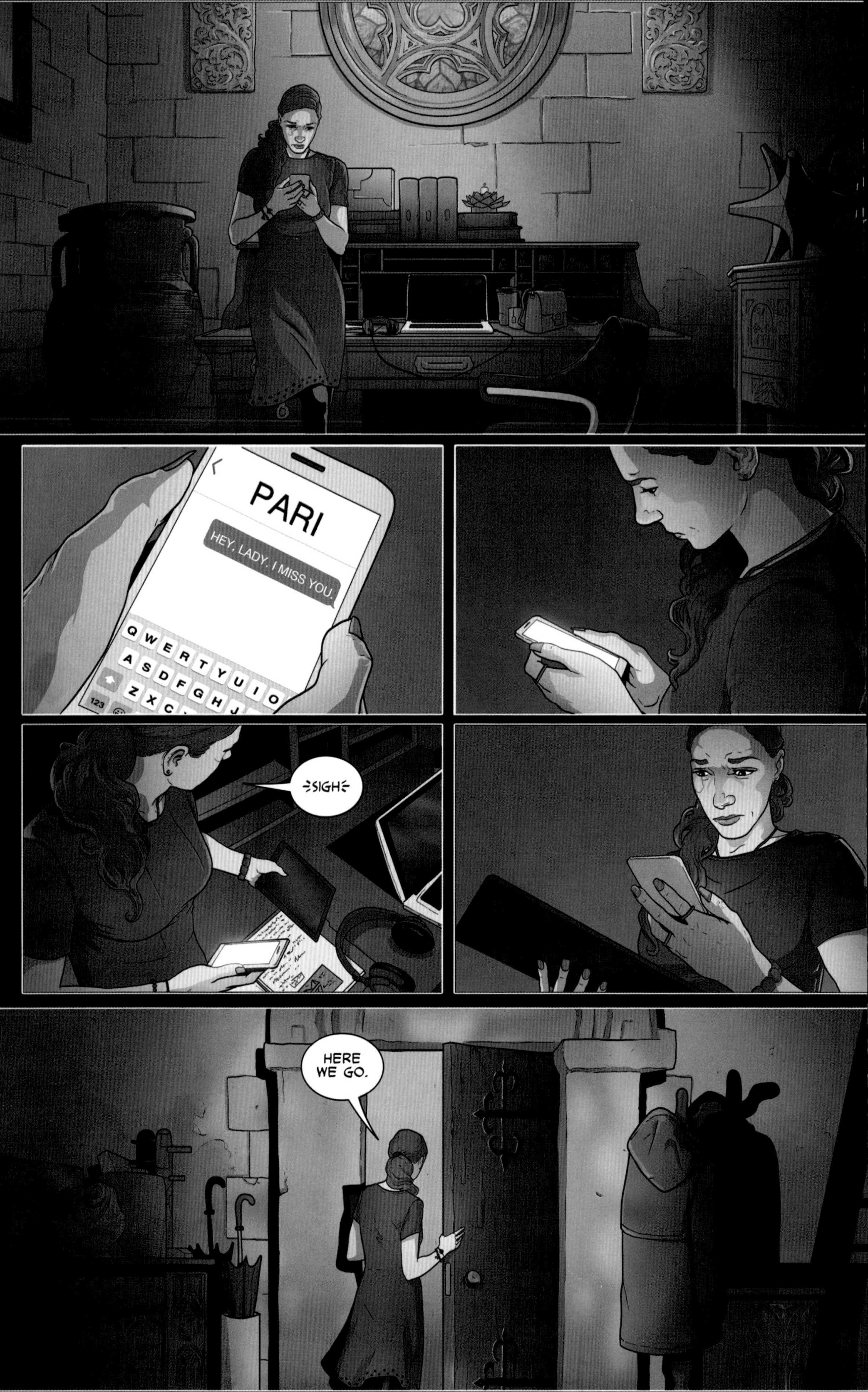
PARI
HEY, LADY. I MISS YOU.
SIGH
HERE WE GO.

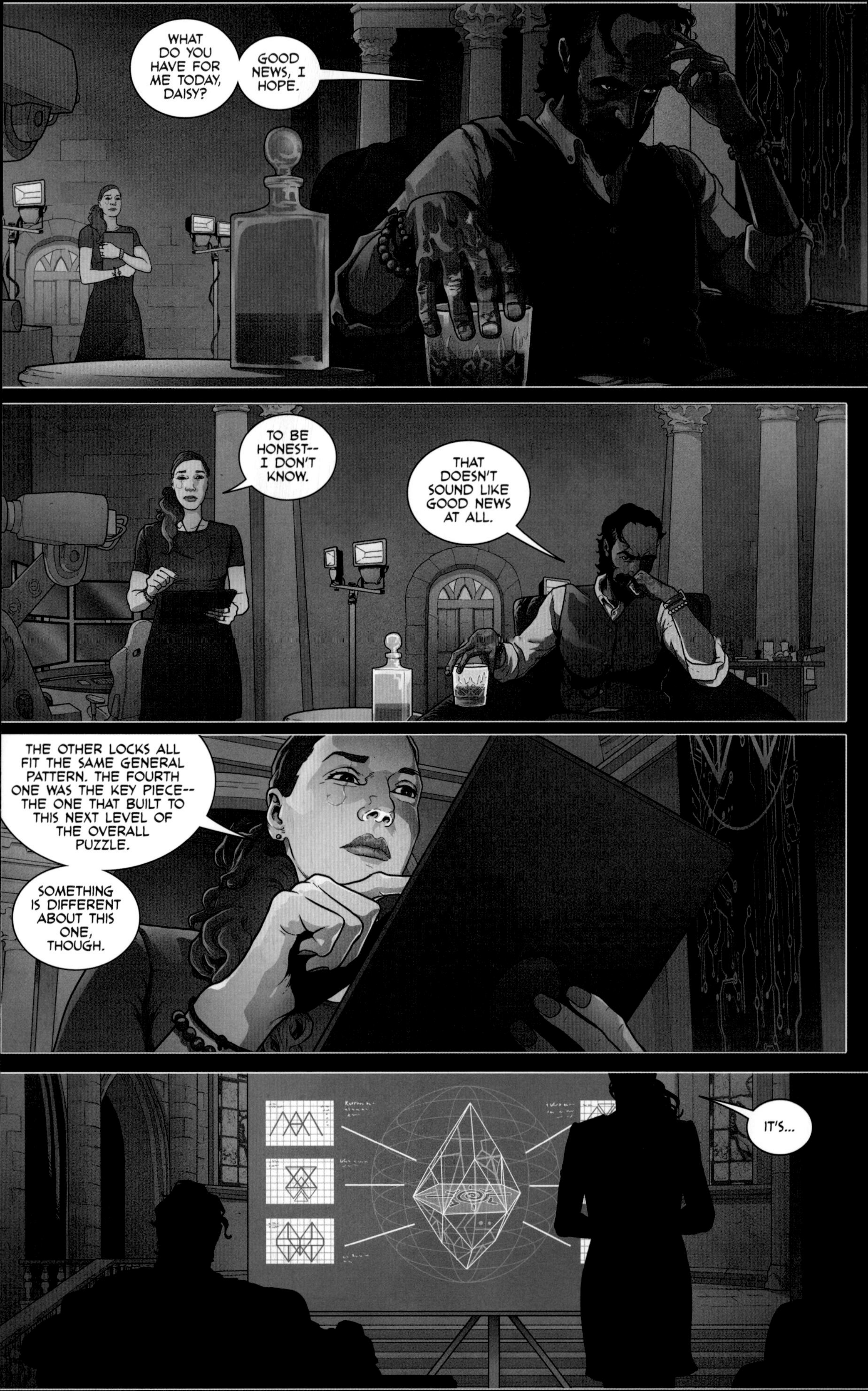
WHAT DO YOU HAVE FOR ME TODAY, DAISY?
GOOD NEWS, I HOPE.
TO BE HONEST-- I DON'T KNOW.
THAT DOESN'T SOUND LIKE GOOD NEWS AT ALL.
THE OTHER LOCKS ALL FIT THE SAME GENERAL PATTERN. THE FOURTH ONE WAS THE KEY PIECE-- THE ONE THAT BUILT TO THIS NEXT LEVEL OF THE OVERALL PUZZLE.
SOMETHING IS DIFFERENT ABOUT THIS ONE, THOUGH.
IT'S...

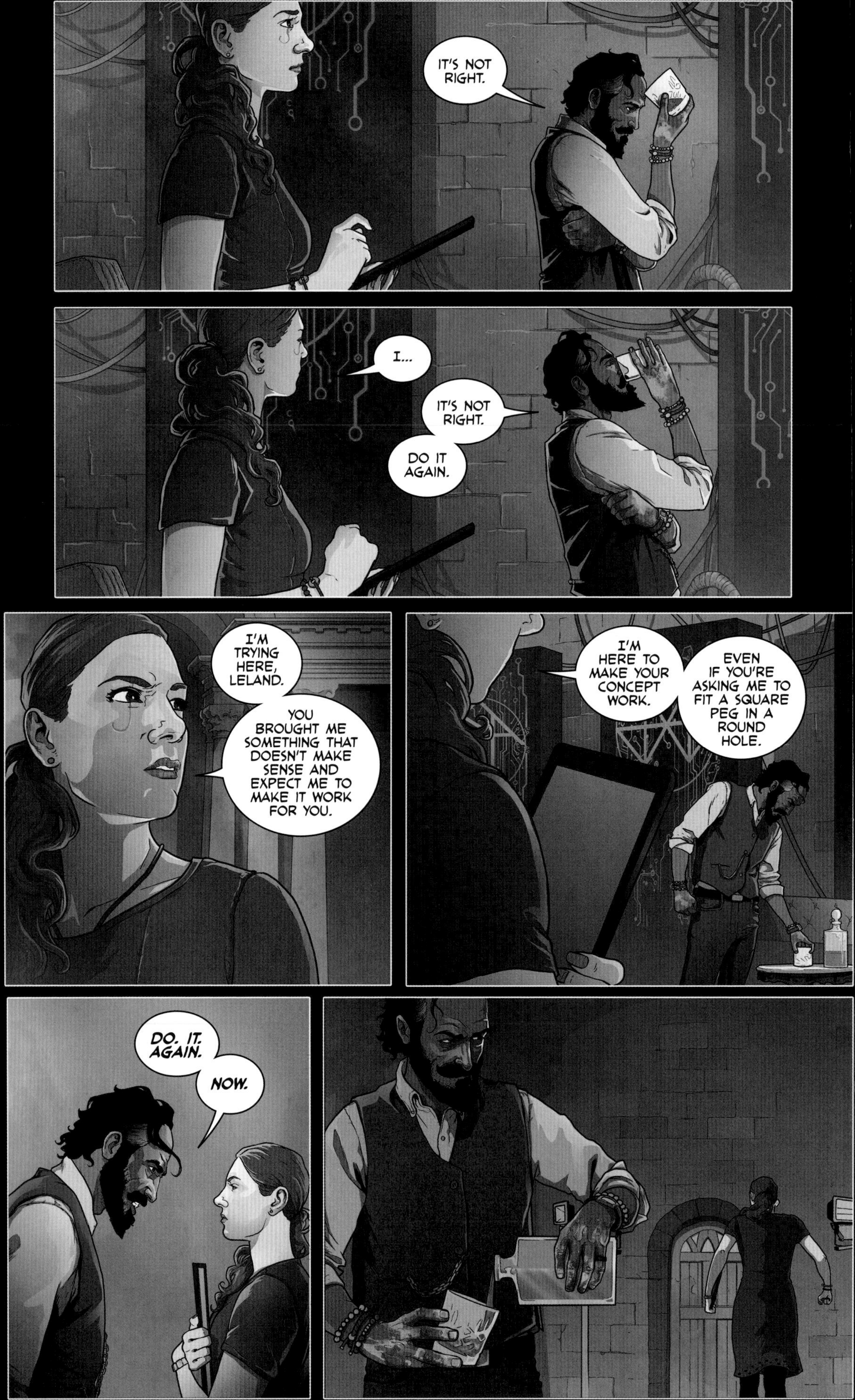
IT'S NOT RIGHT.
I...
IT'S NOT RIGHT.
DO IT AGAIN.
I'M TRYING HERE, LELAND.
YOU BROUGHT ME SOMETHING THAT DOESN'T MAKE SENSE AND EXPECT ME TO MAKE IT WORK FOR YOU.
I'M HERE TO MAKE YOUR CONCEPT WORK.
EVEN IF YOU'RE ASKING ME TO FIT A SQUARE PEG IN A ROUND HOLE.
DO. IT. AGAIN.
NOW.

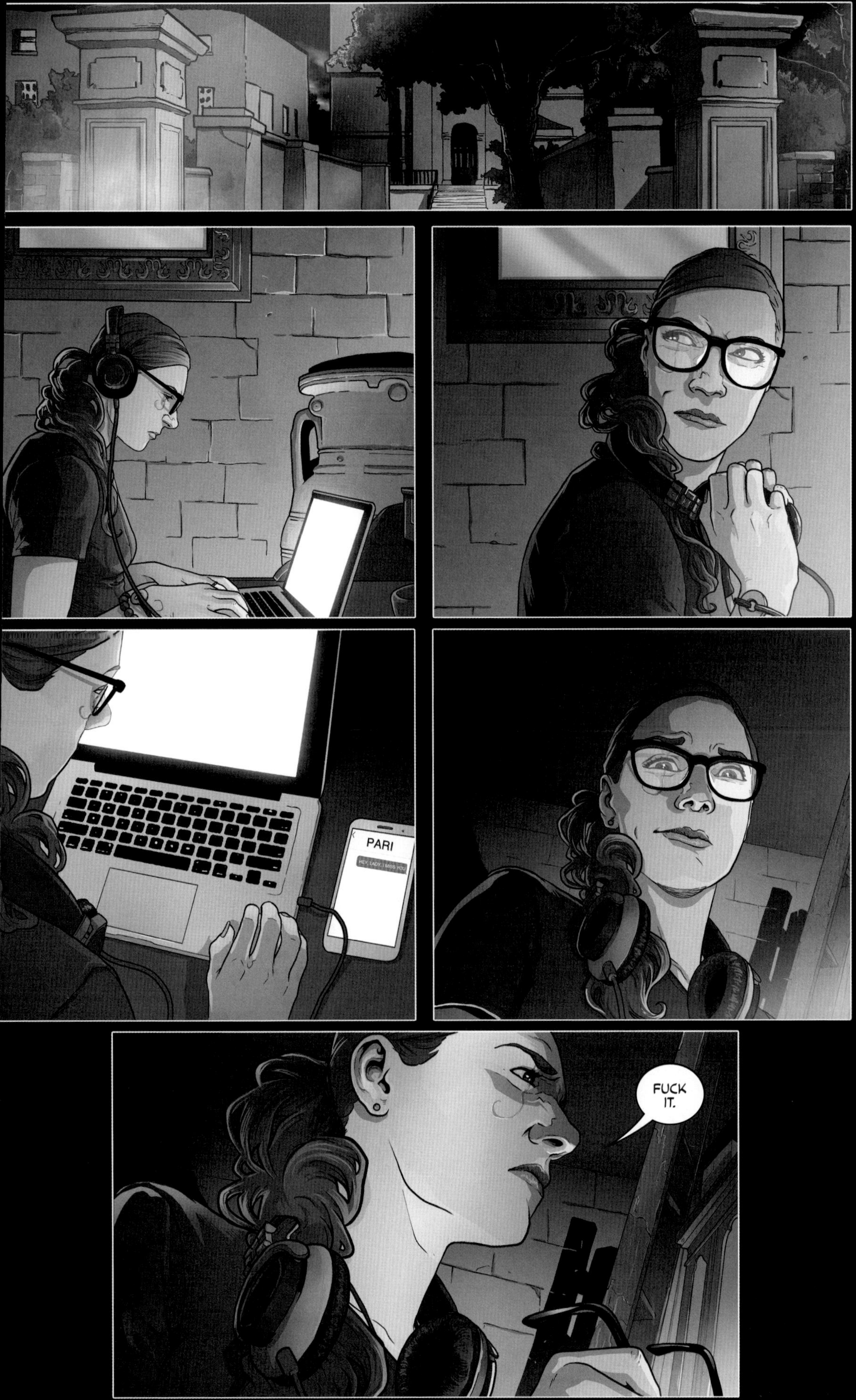
PARI
HEY, LADY. I MISS YOU
FUCK IT.

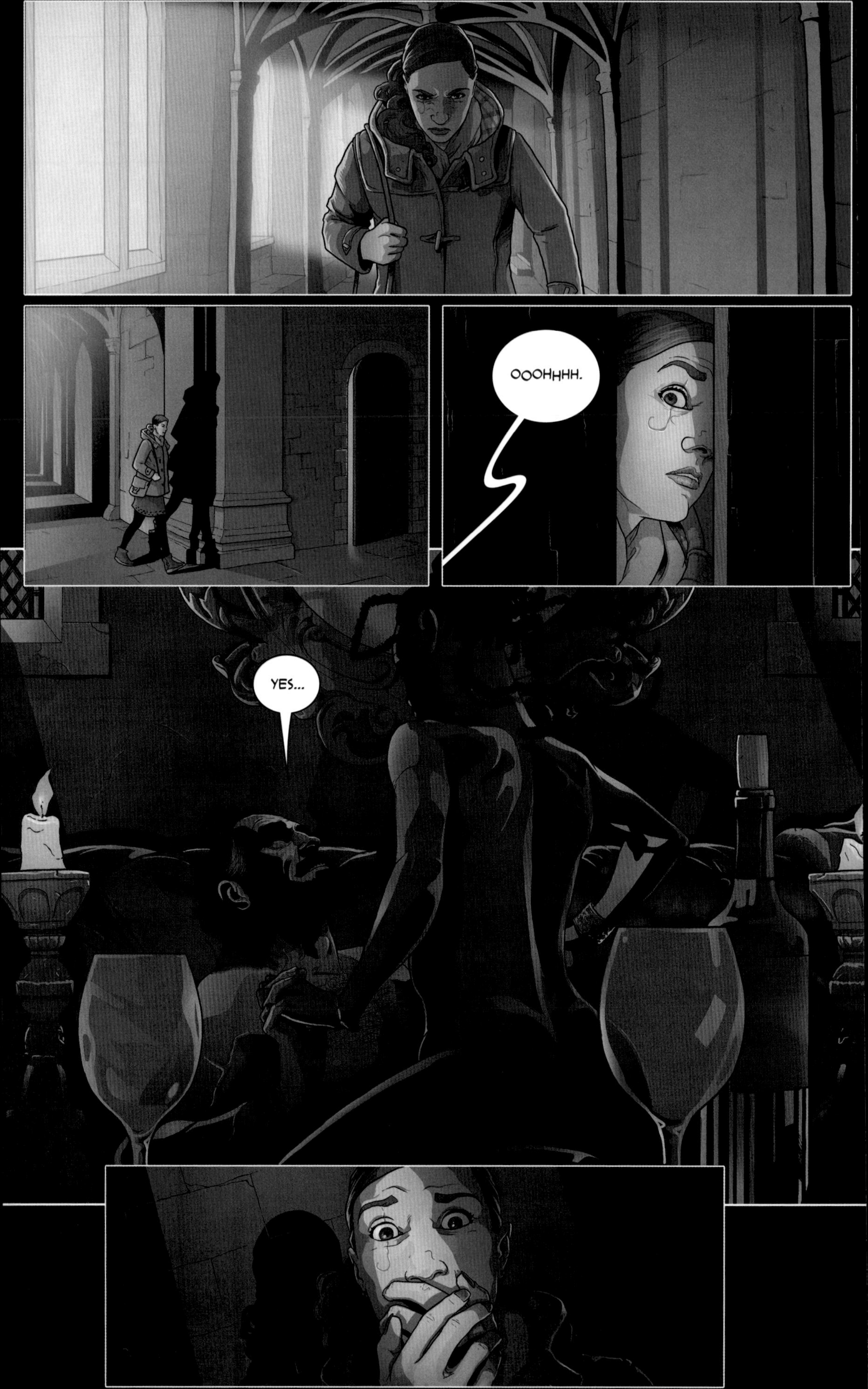
OOOHHHH.
YES...

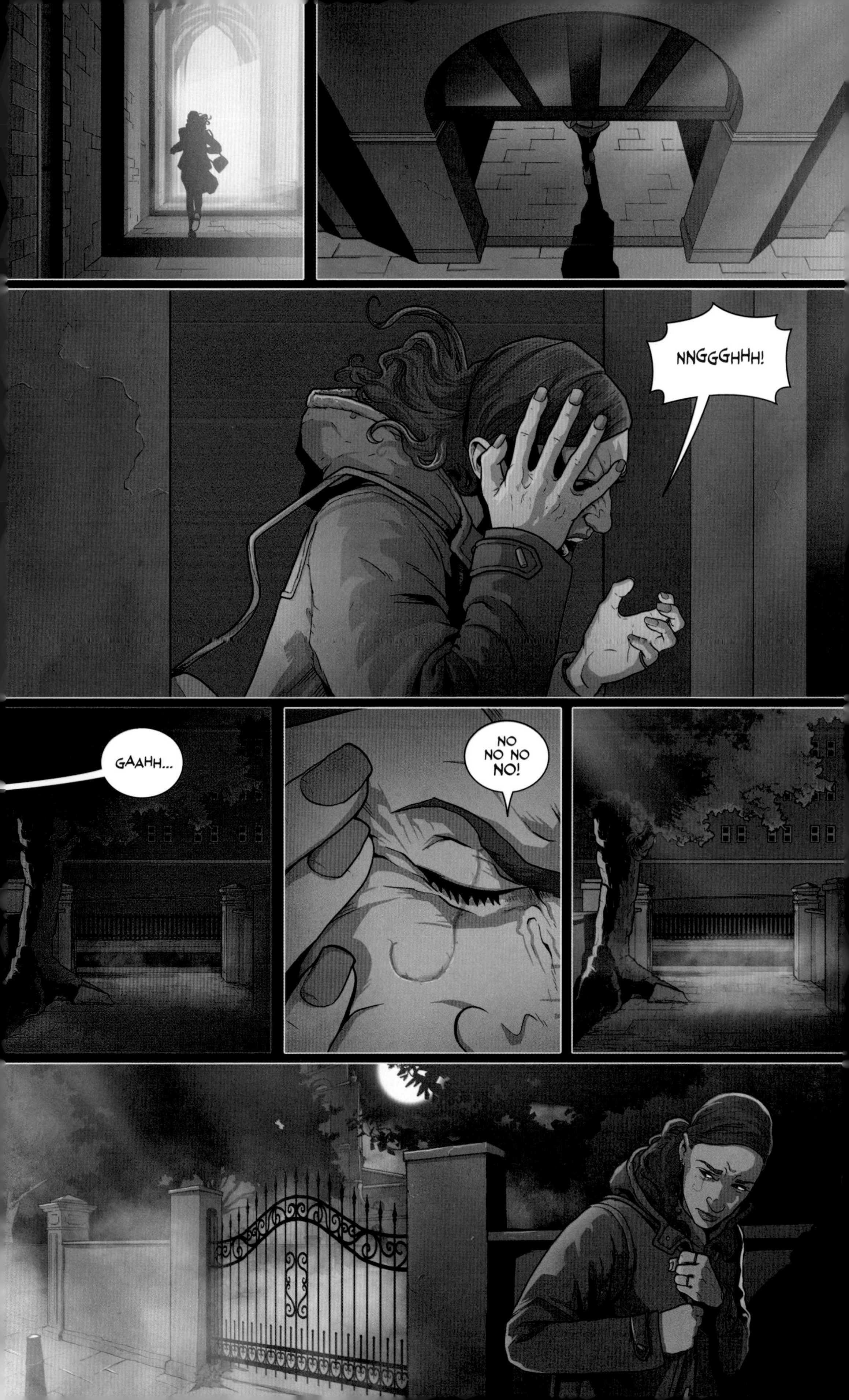
NNGGGHHH!
GAAHH...
NO
NO NO
NO!

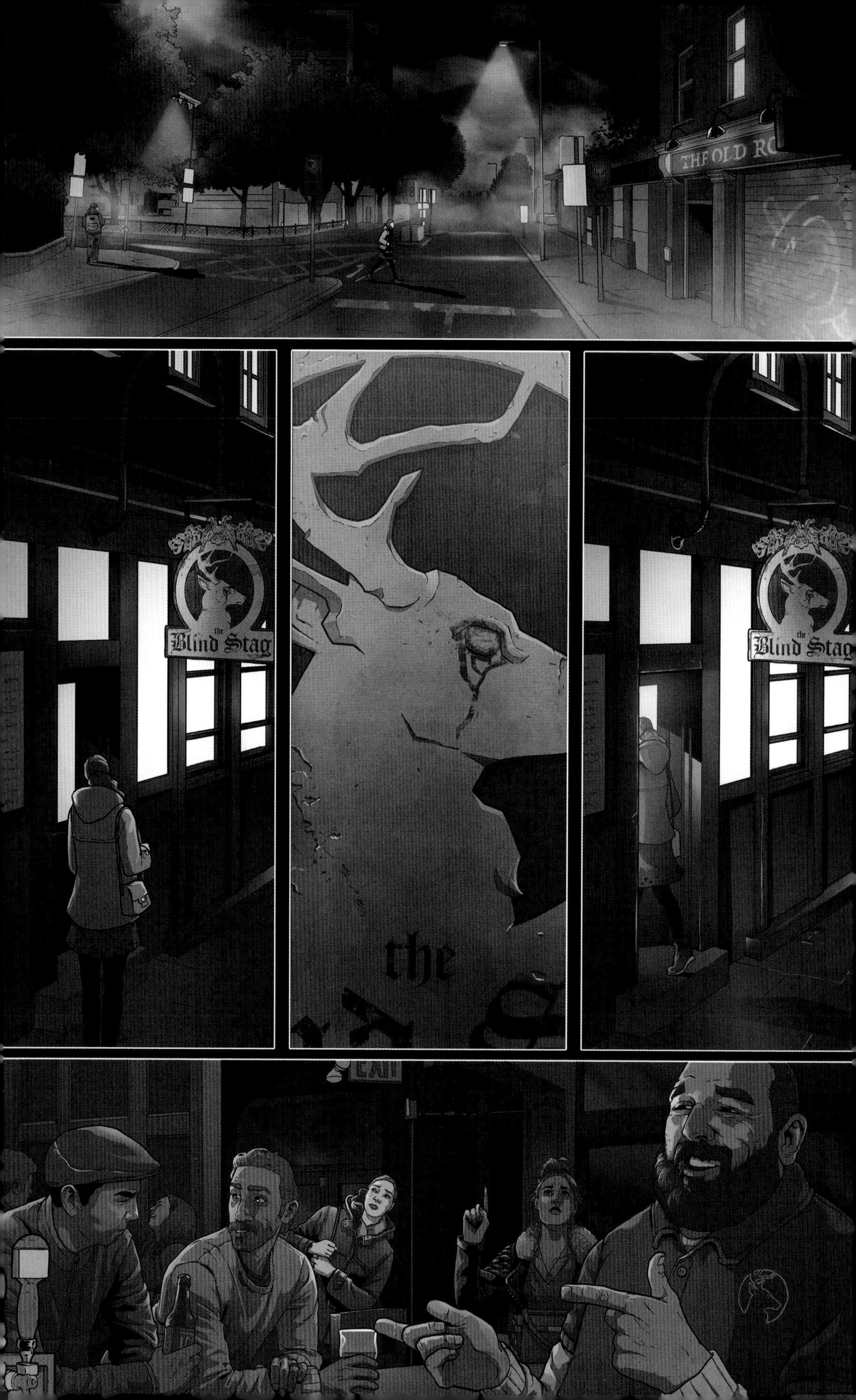
THE OLD RO
the Blind Stag
the
the Blind Stag
EXIT

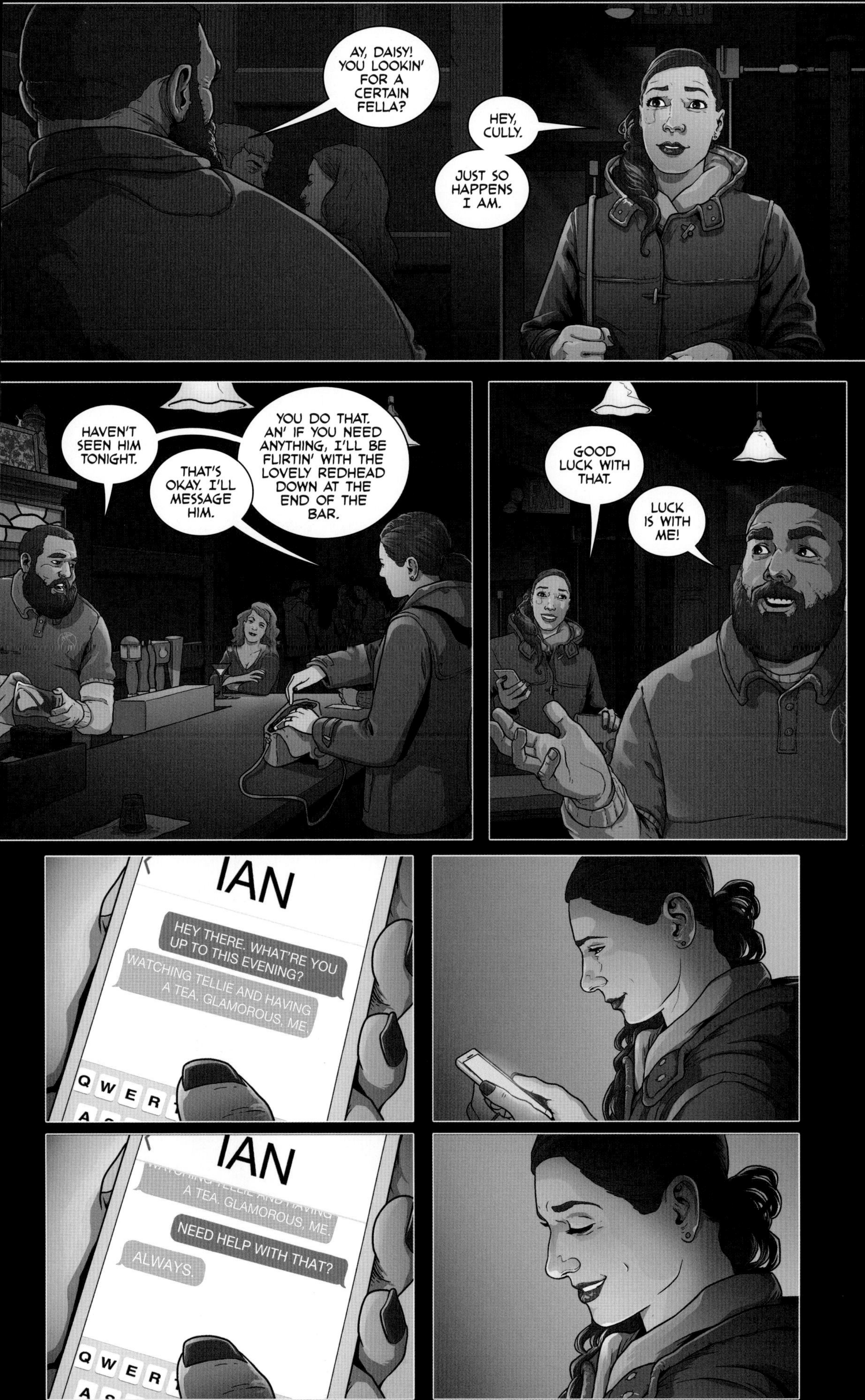
AY, DAISY! YOU LOOKIN' FOR A CERTAIN FELLA?
HEY, CULLY.
JUST SO HAPPENS I AM.
HAVEN'T SEEN HIM TONIGHT.
THAT'S OKAY. I'LL MESSAGE HIM.
YOU DO THAT. AN' IF YOU NEED ANYTHING, I'LL BE FLIRTIN' WITH THE LOVELY REDHEAD DOWN AT THE END OF THE BAR.
GOOD LUCK WITH THAT.
LUCK IS WITH ME!
IAN
HEY THERE. WHAT'RE YOU UP TO THIS EVENING?
WATCHING TELLIE AND HAVING A TEA. GLAMOROUS, ME.
IAN
A TEA. GLAMOROUS, ME.
NEED HELP WITH THAT?
ALWAYS.

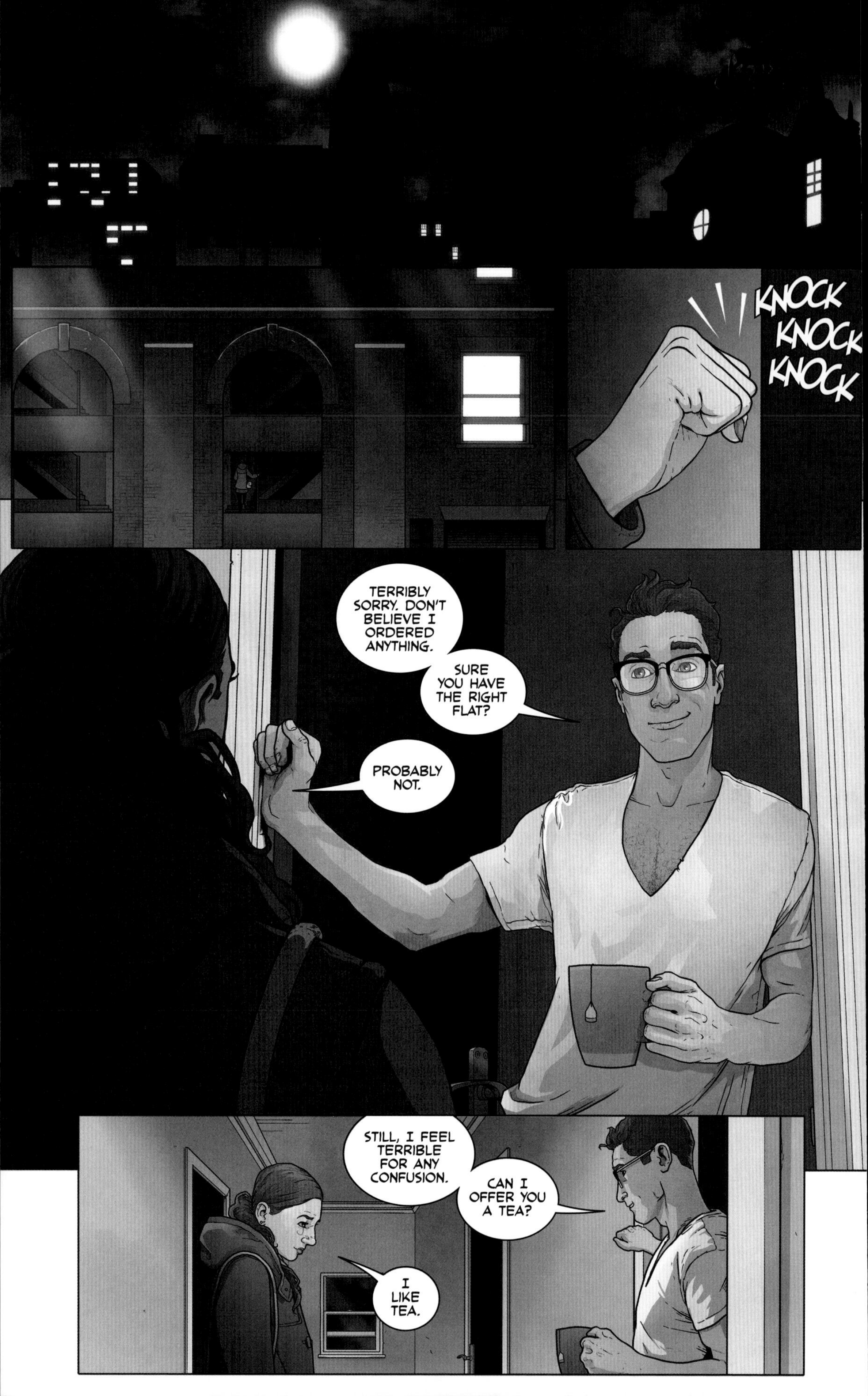
KNOCK KNOCK KNOCK
TERRIBLY SORRY. DON'T BELIEVE I ORDERED ANYTHING.
SURE YOU HAVE THE RIGHT FLAT?
PROBABLY NOT.
STILL, I FEEL TERRIBLE FOR ANY CONFUSION.
CAN I OFFER YOU A TEA?
I LIKE TEA.

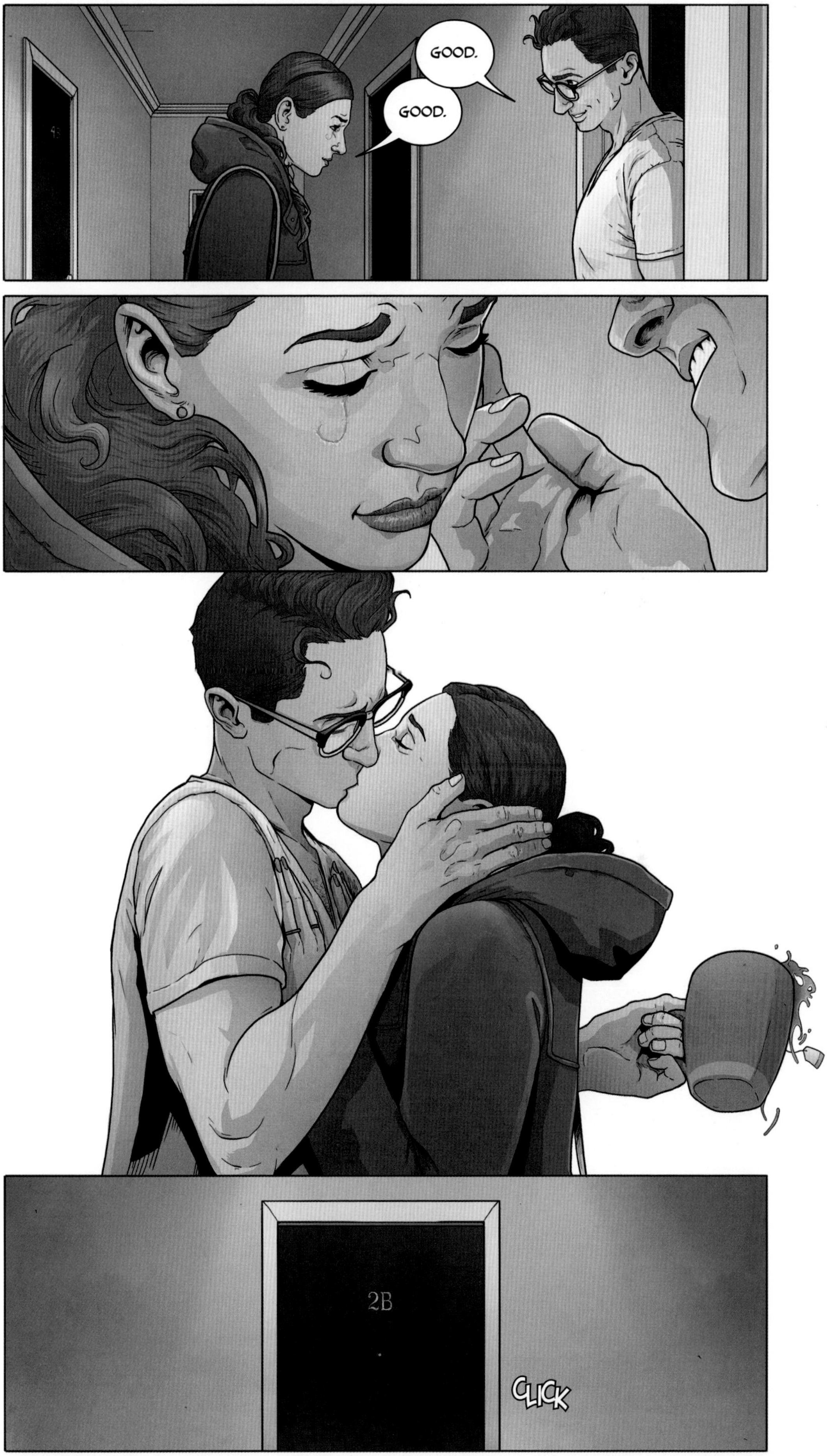
GOOD.
GOOD.
2B
CLICK

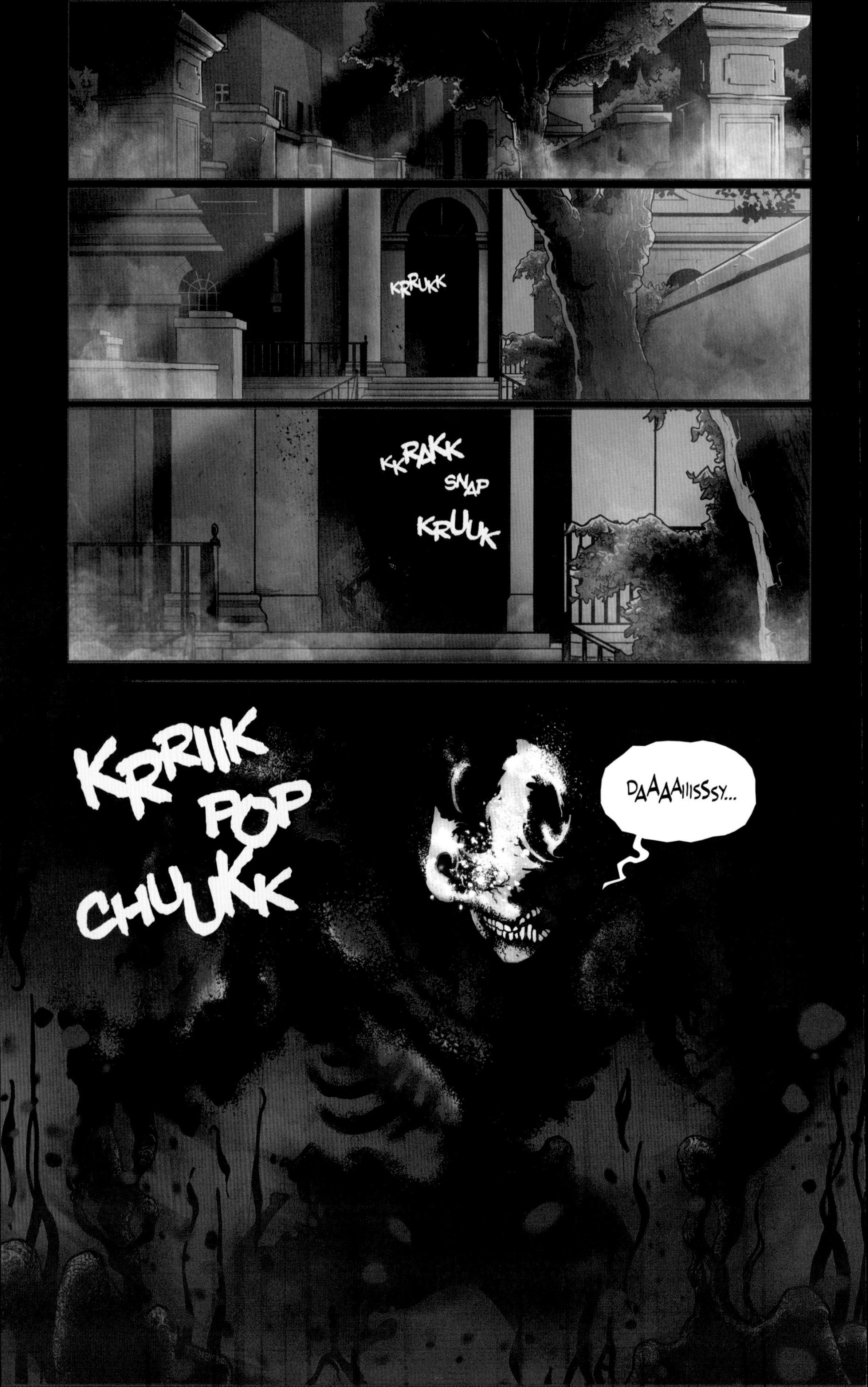
KRRUKK
KKRAKK
SNAP
KRUUK
KRRIIK
POP
CHUUKK
DAAAAIIISSSY...

CHAPTER
EIGHT

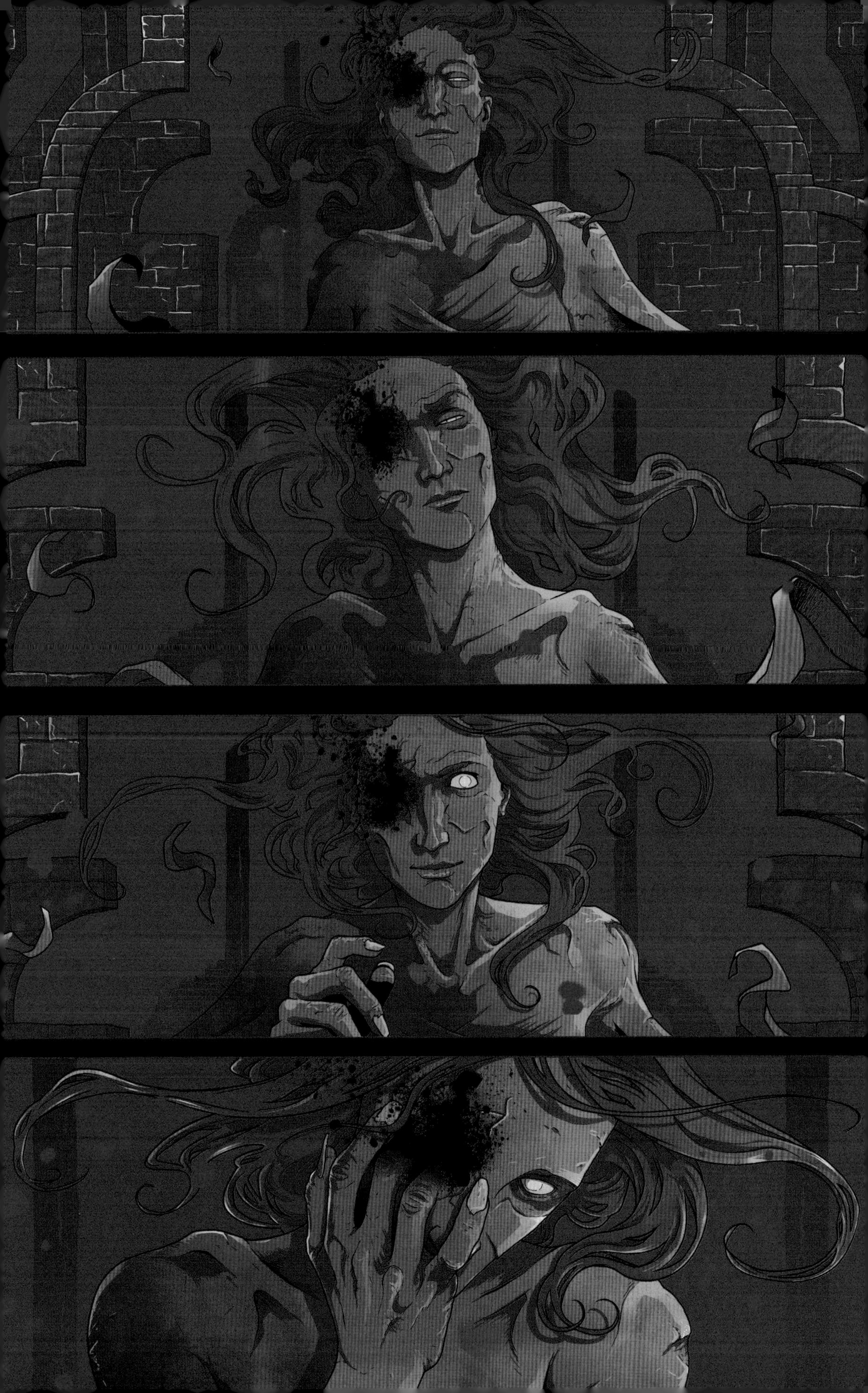

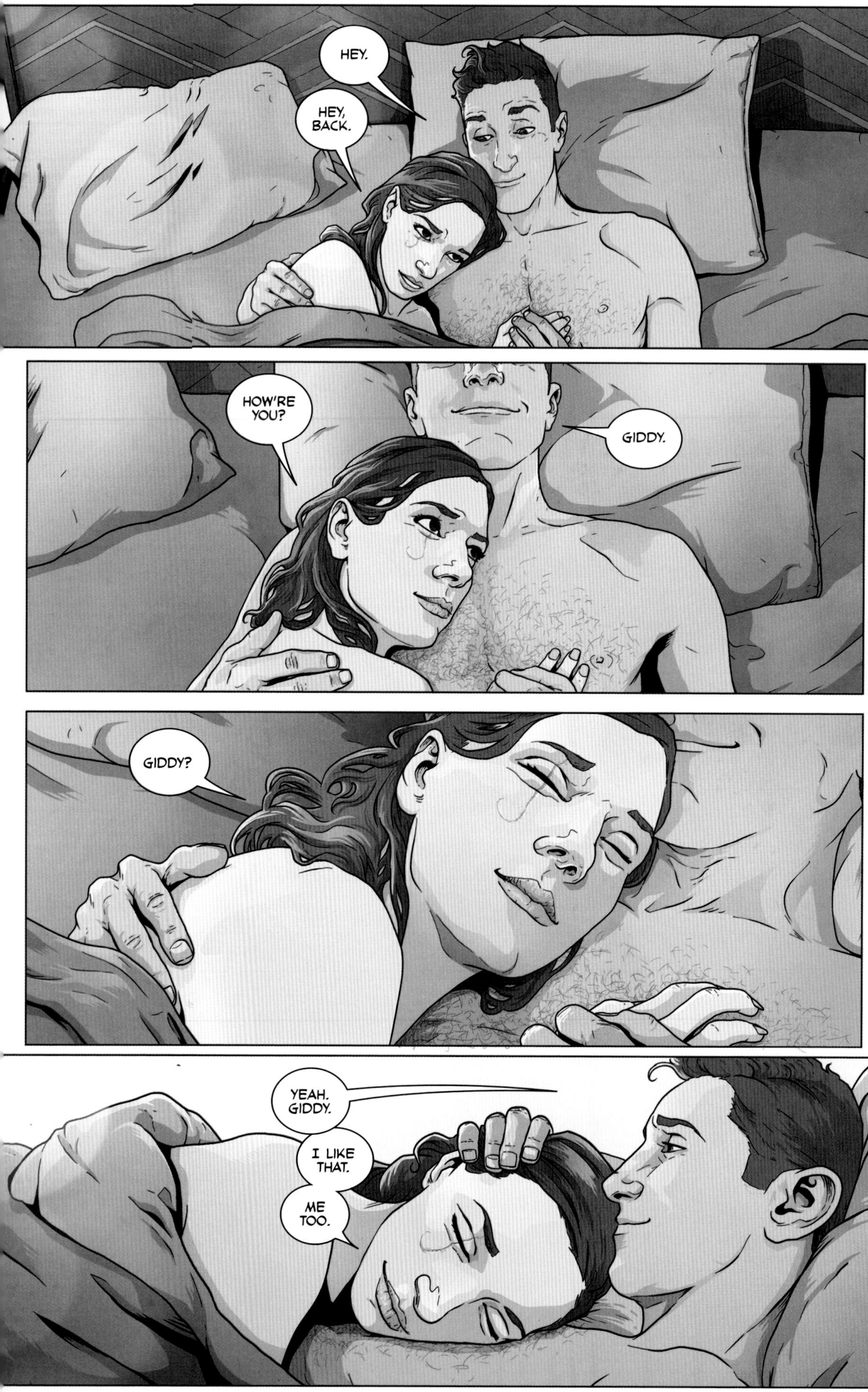
HEY.
HEY, BACK.
HOW'RE YOU?
GIDDY.
GIDDY?
YEAH. GIDDY.
I LIKE THAT.
ME TOO.

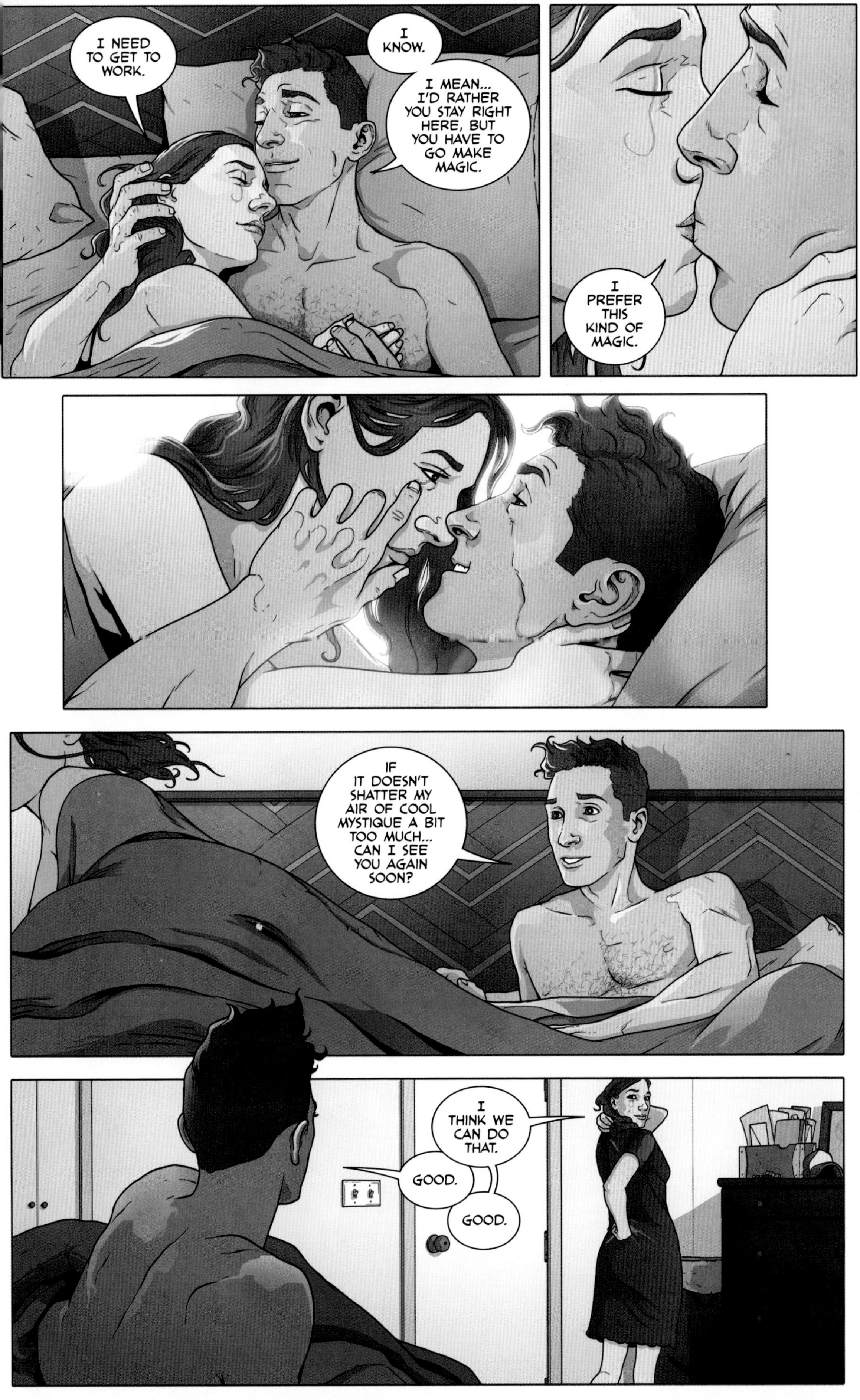
I NEED TO GET TO WORK.
I KNOW.
I MEAN... I'D RATHER YOU STAY RIGHT HERE, BUT YOU HAVE TO GO MAKE MAGIC.
I PREFER THIS KIND OF MAGIC.
IF IT DOESN'T SHATTER MY AIR OF COOL MYSTIQUE A BIT TOO MUCH... CAN I SEE YOU AGAIN SOON?
I THINK WE CAN DO THAT.
GOOD.
GOOD.

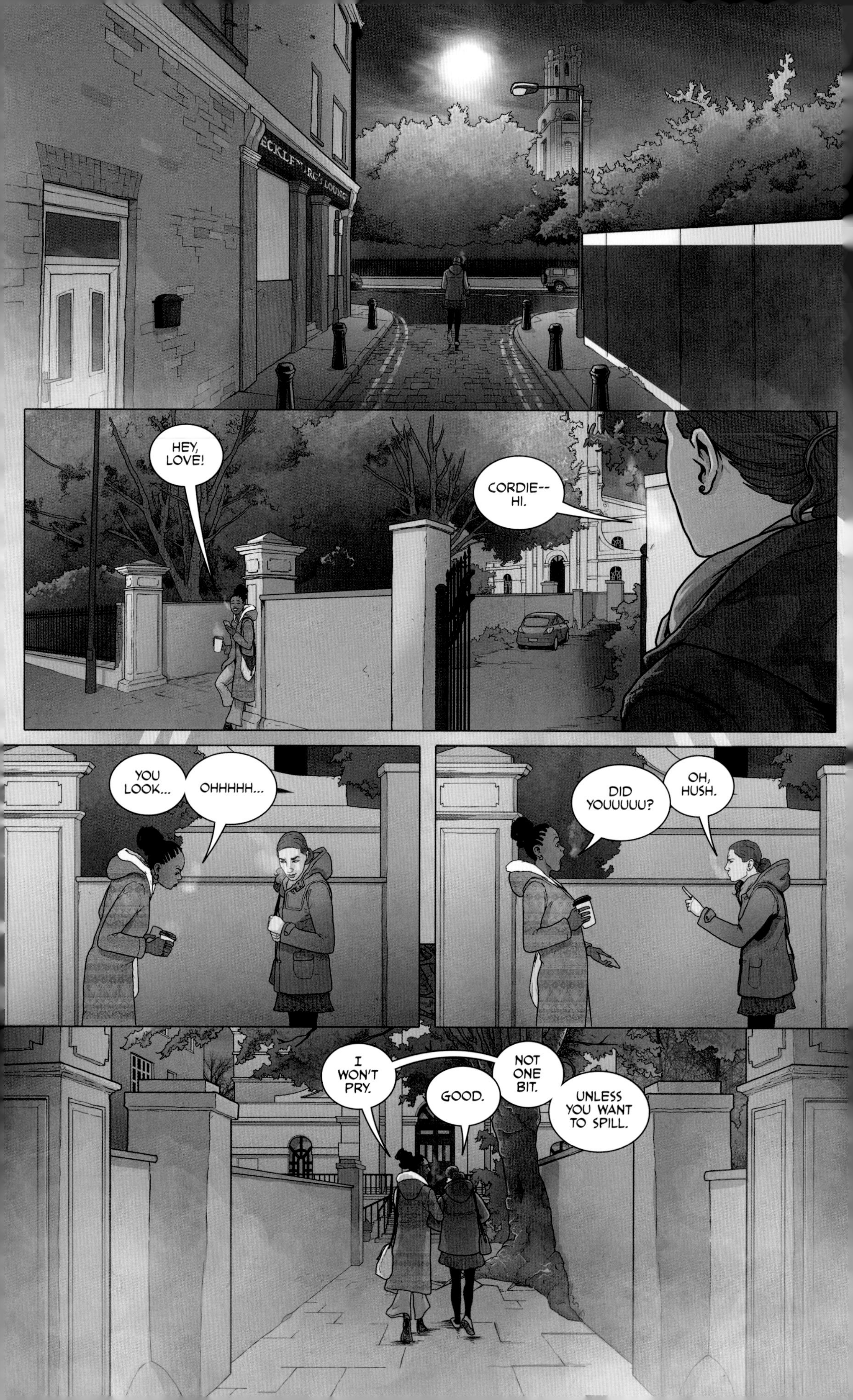
HEY, LOVE!
CORDIE-- HI.
YOU LOOK...
OHHHHH...
DID YOUUUUU?
OH, HUSH.
I WON'T PRY.
NOT ONE BIT.
GOOD.
UNLESS YOU WANT TO SPILL.

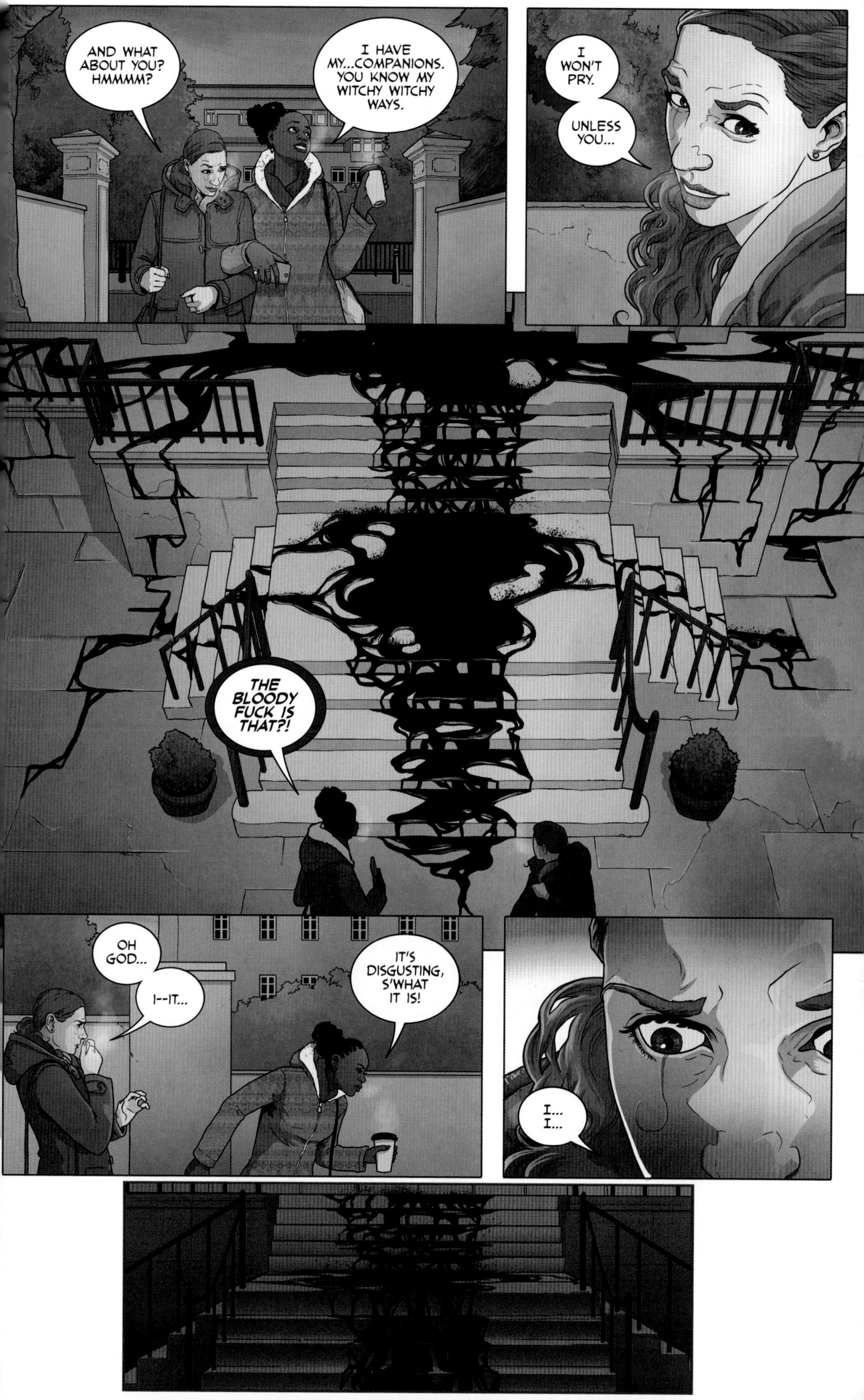
AND WHAT ABOUT YOU? HMMMM?
I HAVE MY...COMPANIONS. YOU KNOW MY WITCHY WITCHY WAYS.
I WON'T PRY.
UNLESS YOU...
THE BLOODY FUCK IS THAT?!
OH GOD...
I--IT...
IT'S DISGUSTING, S'WHAT IT IS!
I... I...

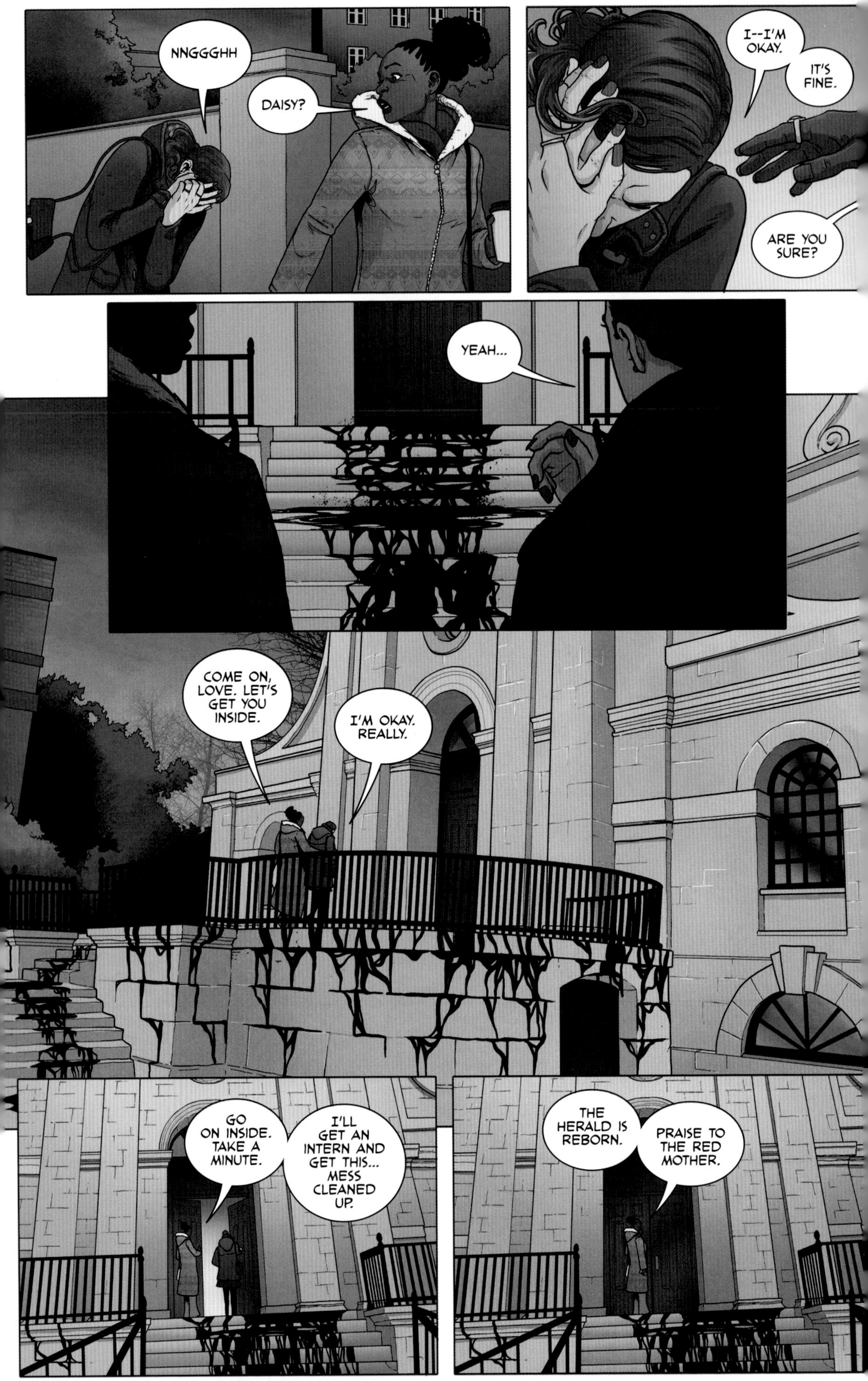
NNGGGHH
DAISY?
I--I'M OKAY.
IT'S FINE.
ARE YOU SURE?
YEAH...
COME ON, LOVE. LET'S GET YOU INSIDE.
I'M OKAY. REALLY.
GO ON INSIDE. TAKE A MINUTE.
I'LL GET AN INTERN AND GET THIS... MESS CLEANED UP.
THE HERALD IS REBORN.
PRAISE TO THE RED MOTHER.

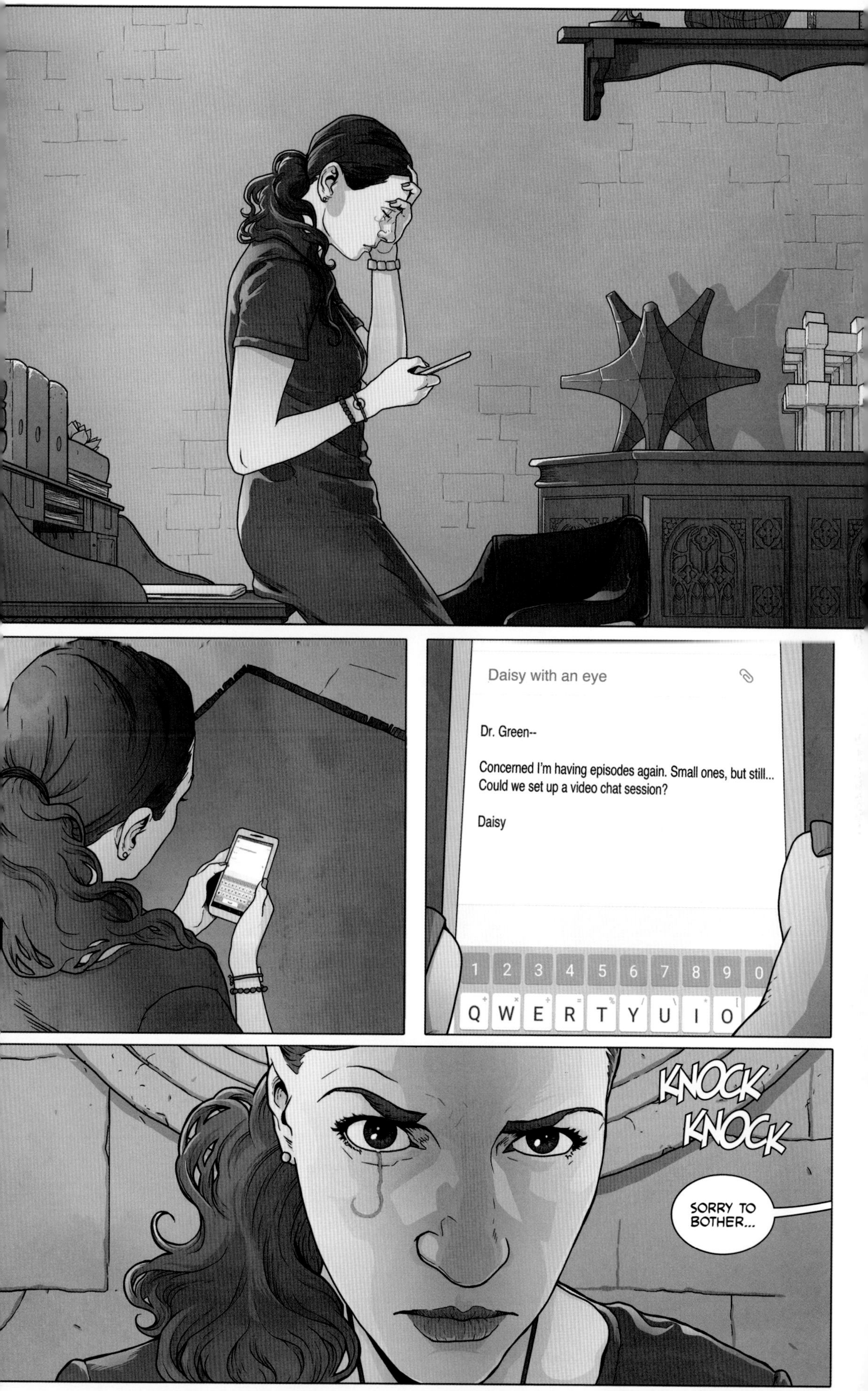
Daisy with an eye
Dr. Green--
Concerned I'm having episodes again. Small ones, but still...
Could we set up a video chat session?
Daisy
1 2 3 4 5 6 7 8 9 0
Q W E R T Y U I O
KNOCK KNOCK
SORRY TO BOTHER...

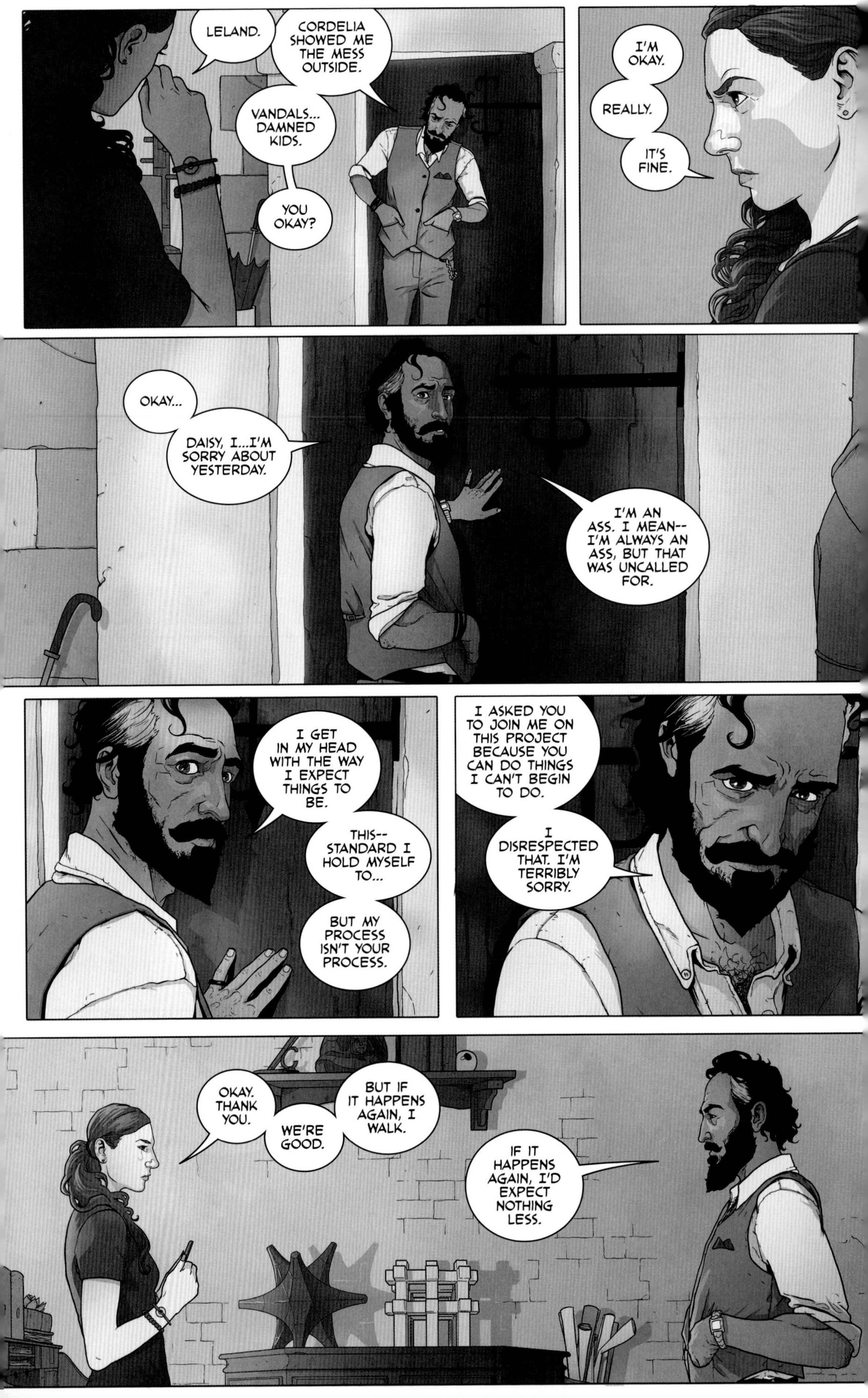
LELAND.
CORDELIA SHOWED ME THE MESS OUTSIDE.
VANDALS... DAMNED KIDS.
YOU OKAY?
I'M OKAY.
REALLY.
IT'S FINE.
OKAY...
DAISY, I...I'M SORRY ABOUT YESTERDAY.
I'M AN ASS. I MEAN-- I'M ALWAYS AN ASS, BUT THAT WAS UNCALLED FOR.
I GET IN MY HEAD WITH THE WAY I EXPECT THINGS TO BE.
THIS-- STANDARD I HOLD MYSELF TO...
BUT MY PROCESS ISN'T YOUR PROCESS.
I ASKED YOU TO JOIN ME ON THIS PROJECT BECAUSE YOU CAN DO THINGS I CAN'T BEGIN TO DO.
I DISRESPECTED THAT. I'M TERRIBLY SORRY.
OKAY. THANK YOU.
WE'RE GOOD.
BUT IF IT HAPPENS AGAIN, I WALK.
IF IT HAPPENS AGAIN, I'D EXPECT NOTHING LESS.

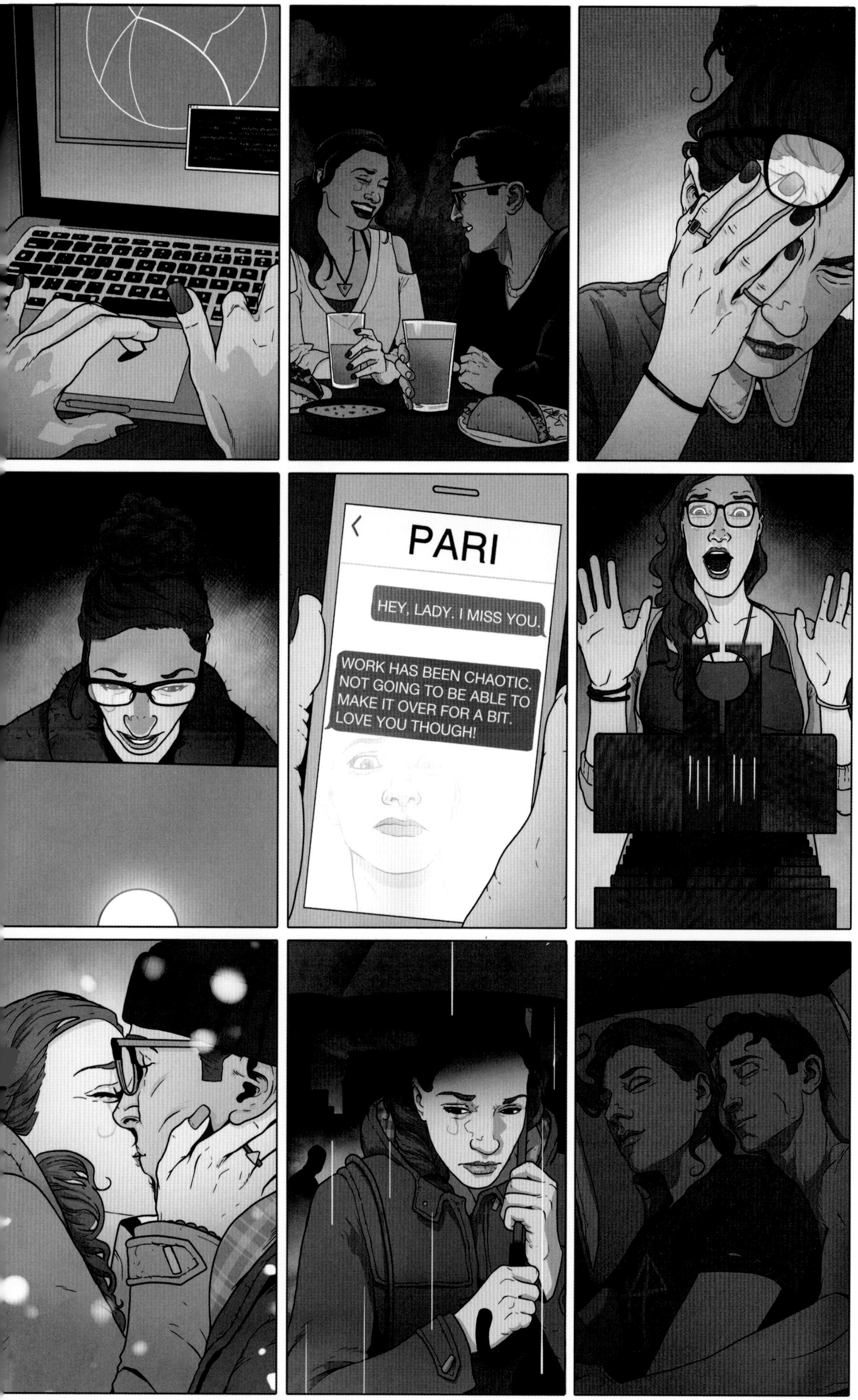
PARI
HEY, LADY. I MISS YOU.
WORK HAS BEEN CHAOTIC. NOT GOING TO BE ABLE TO MAKE IT OVER FOR A BIT. LOVE YOU THOUGH!

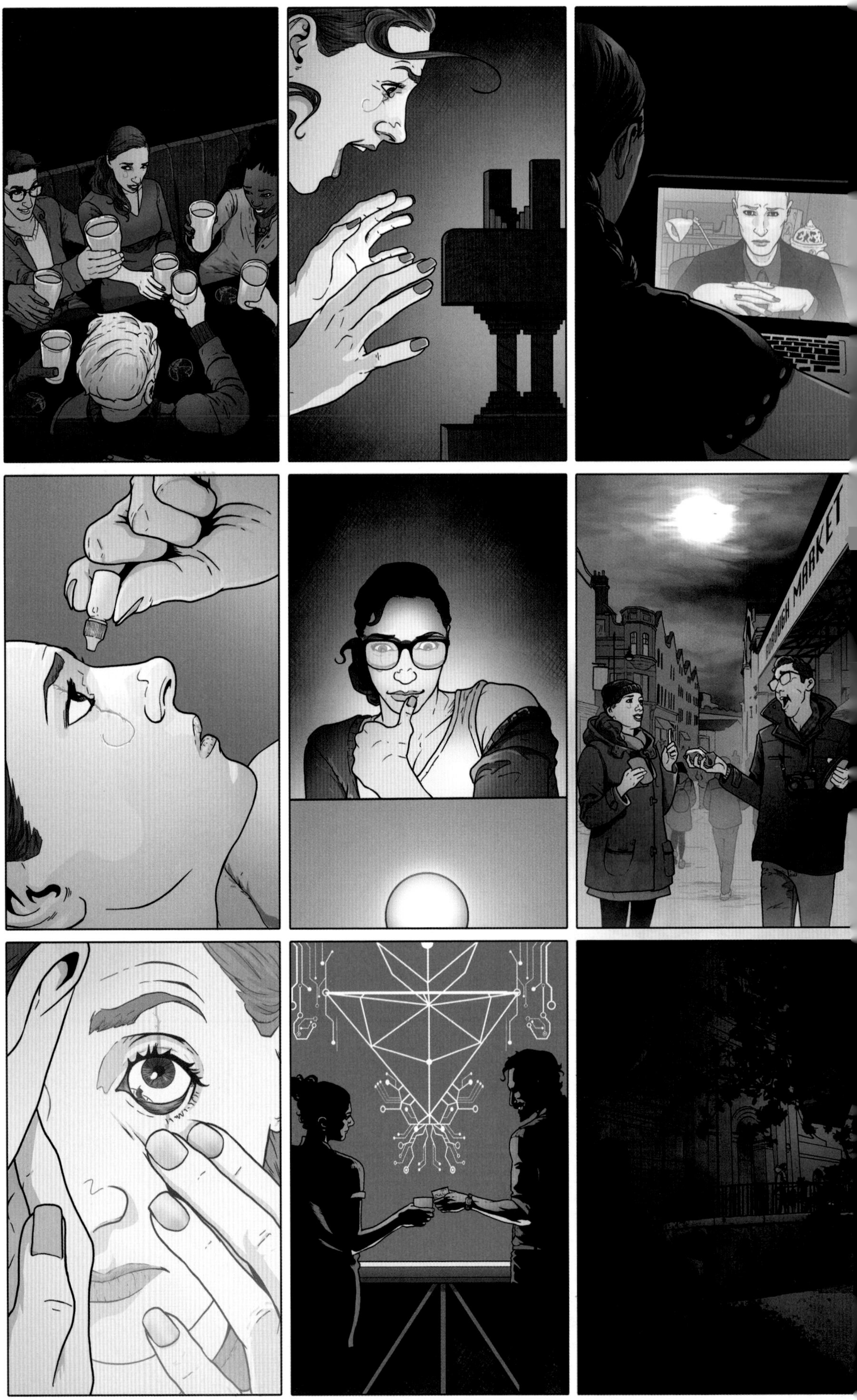
BOROUGH MARKET

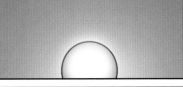

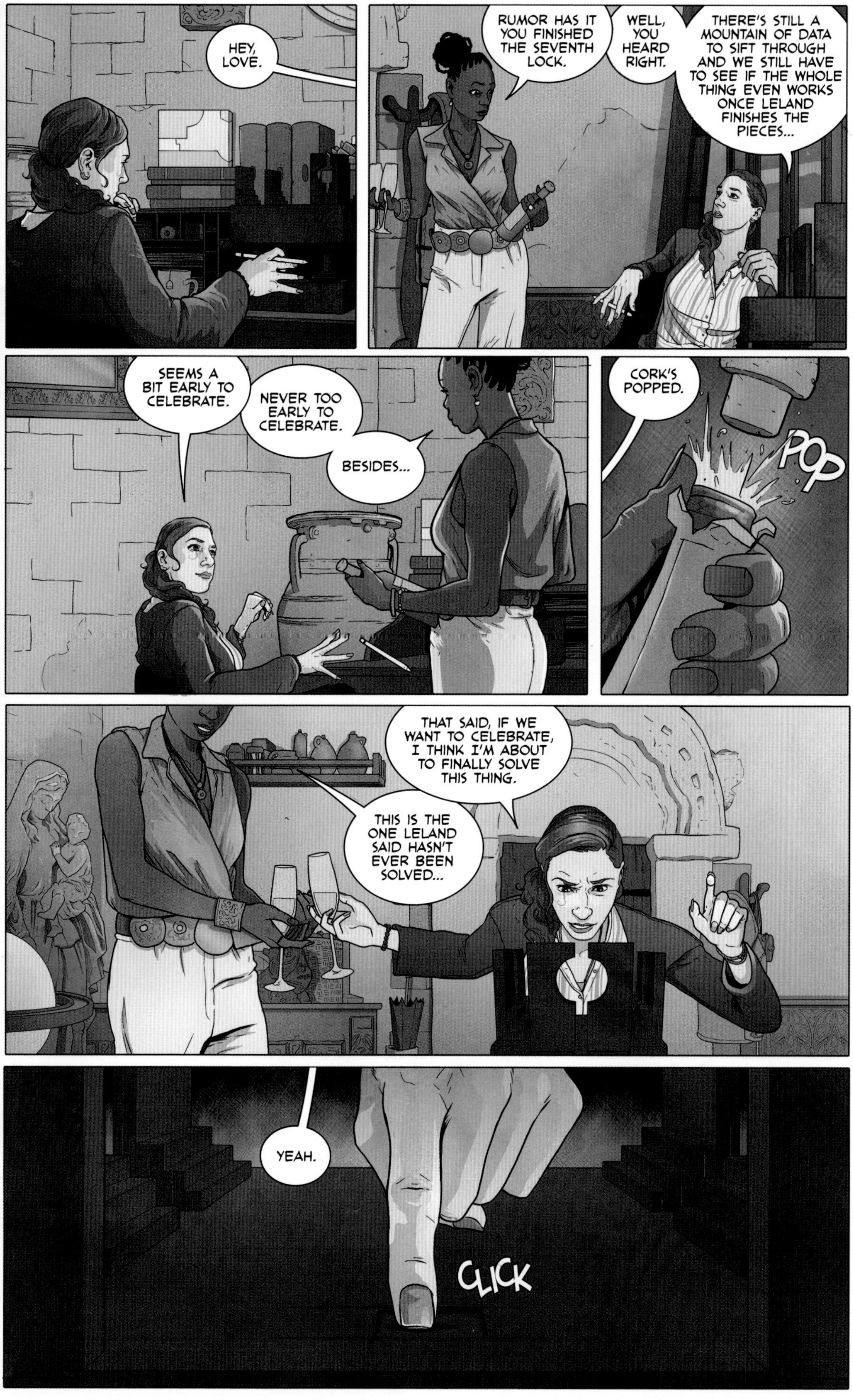
HEY, LOVE.
RUMOR HAS IT YOU FINISHED THE SEVENTH LOCK.
WELL, YOU HEARD RIGHT.
THERE'S STILL A MOUNTAIN OF DATA TO SIFT THROUGH AND WE STILL HAVE TO SEE IF THE WHOLE THING EVEN WORKS ONCE LELAND FINISHES THE PIECES...
SEEMS A BIT EARLY TO CELEBRATE.
NEVER TOO EARLY TO CELEBRATE.
BESIDES...
CORK'S POPPED.
POP
THAT SAID, IF WE WANT TO CELEBRATE, I THINK I'M ABOUT TO FINALLY SOLVE THIS THING.
THIS IS THE ONE LELAND SAID HASN'T EVER BEEN SOLVED...
YEAH.
CLICK

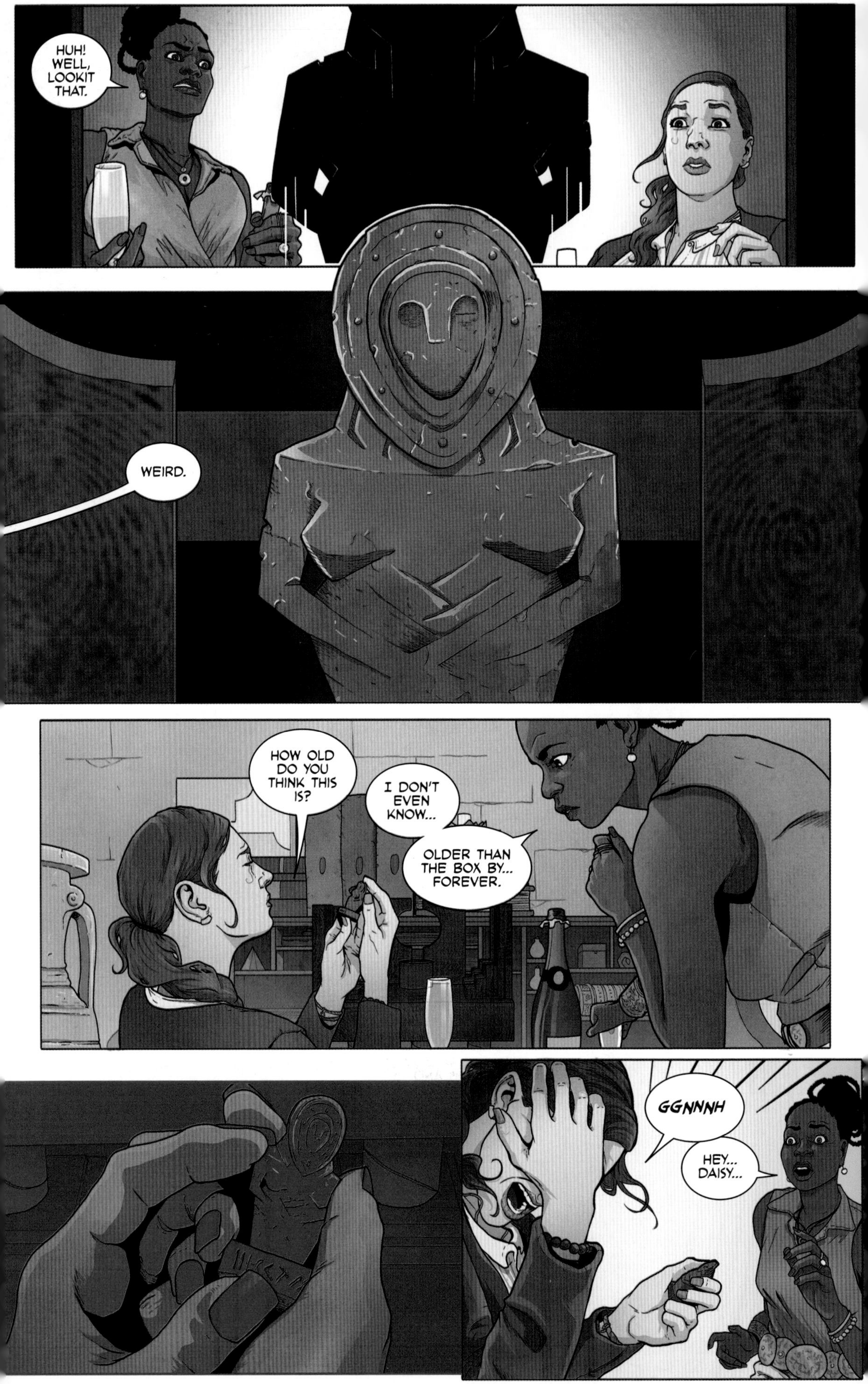
HUH! WELL, LOOKIT THAT.
WEIRD.
HOW OLD DO YOU THINK THIS IS?
I DON'T EVEN KNOW...
OLDER THAN THE BOX BY... FOREVER.
GGNNNH
HEY... DAISY...

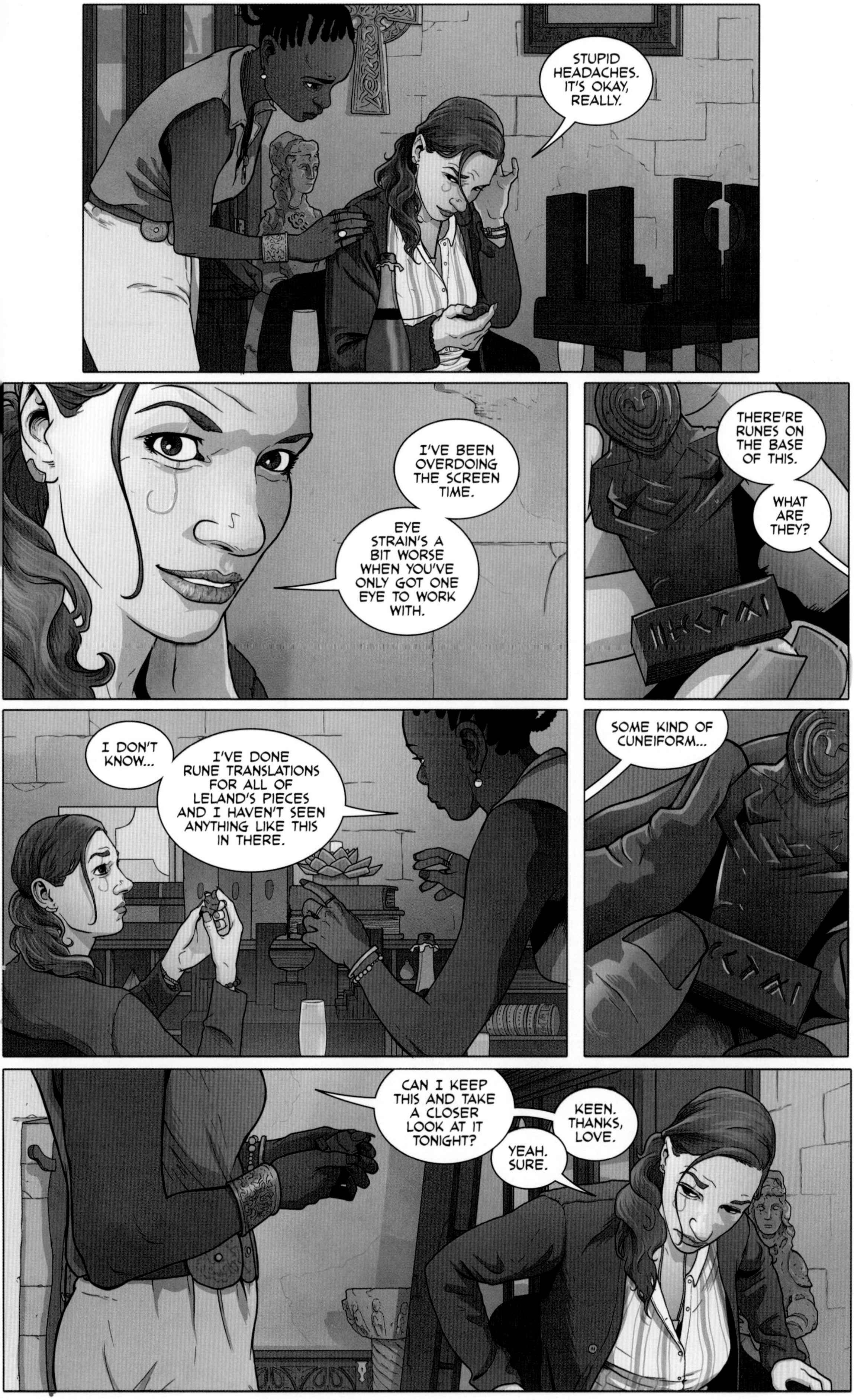
STUPID HEADACHES. IT'S OKAY, REALLY.
I'VE BEEN OVERDOING THE SCREEN TIME.
EYE STRAIN'S A BIT WORSE WHEN YOU'VE ONLY GOT ONE EYE TO WORK WITH.
THERE'RE RUNES ON THE BASE OF THIS.
WHAT ARE THEY?
I DON'T KNOW...
I'VE DONE RUNE TRANSLATIONS FOR ALL OF LELAND'S PIECES AND I HAVEN'T SEEN ANYTHING LIKE THIS IN THERE.
SOME KIND OF CUNEIFORM...
CAN I KEEP THIS AND TAKE A CLOSER LOOK AT IT TONIGHT?
YEAH. SURE.
KEEN. THANKS, LOVE.

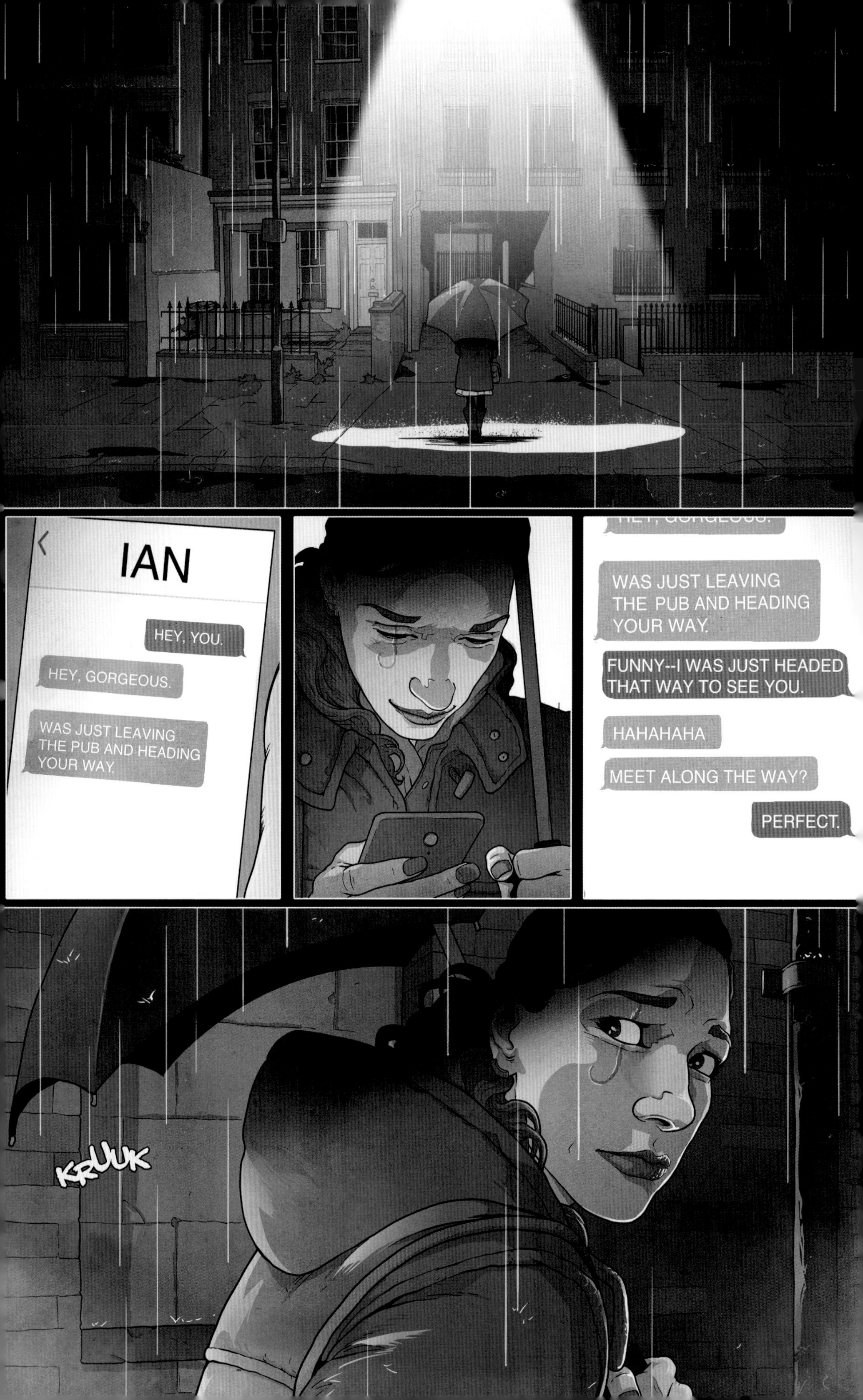

IAN
HEY, YOU.
HEY, GORGEOUS.
WAS JUST LEAVING THE PUB AND HEADING YOUR WAY.
WAS JUST LEAVING THE PUB AND HEADING YOUR WAY.
FUNNY--I WAS JUST HEADED THAT WAY TO SEE YOU.
HAHAHAHA
MEET ALONG THE WAY?
PERFECT.
KRUUK

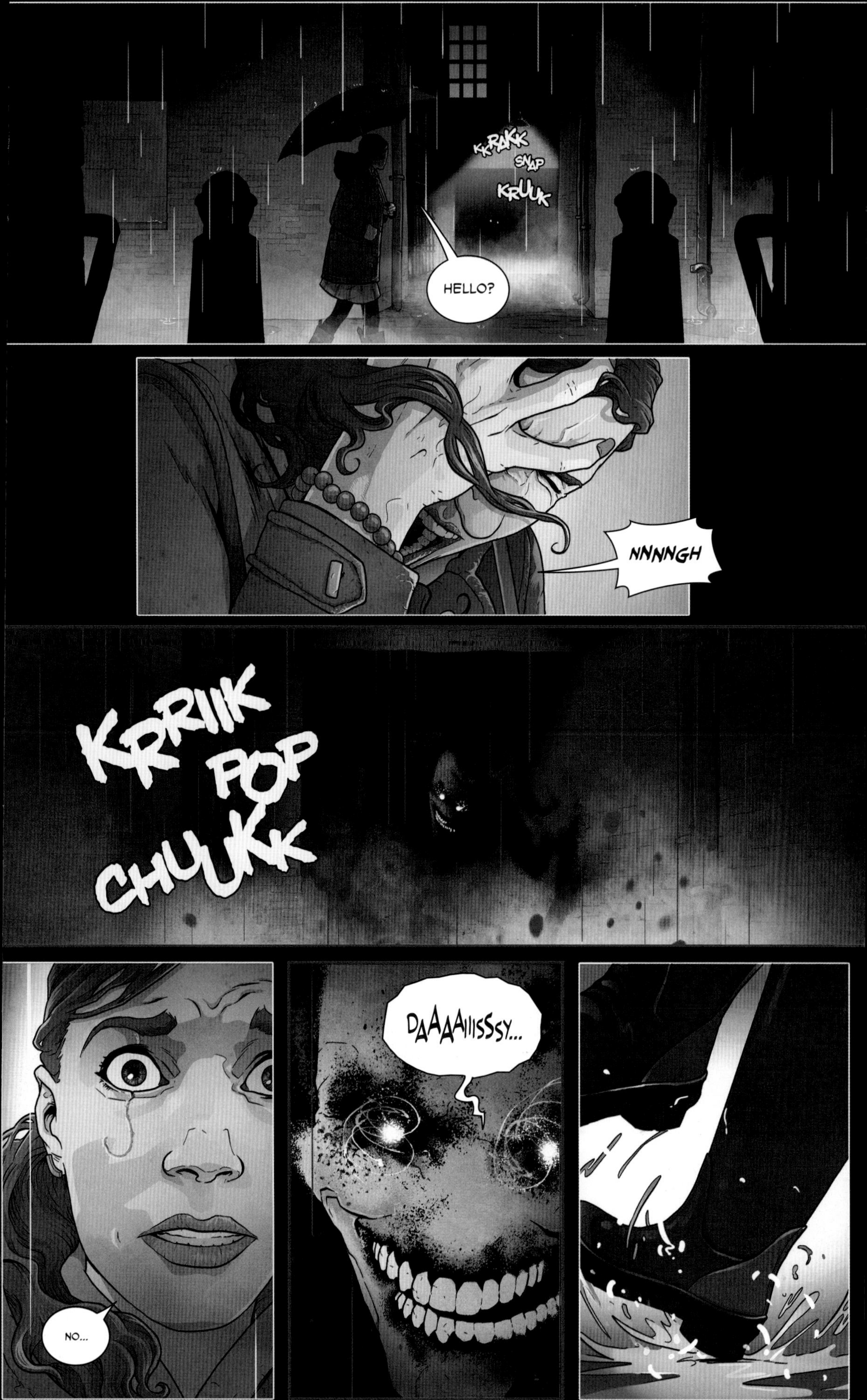
KKRAKK
SNAP
KRUUK
HELLO?
NNNNGH
KRRIIK
POP
CHUKK
NO...
DAAAAIIISSSY...

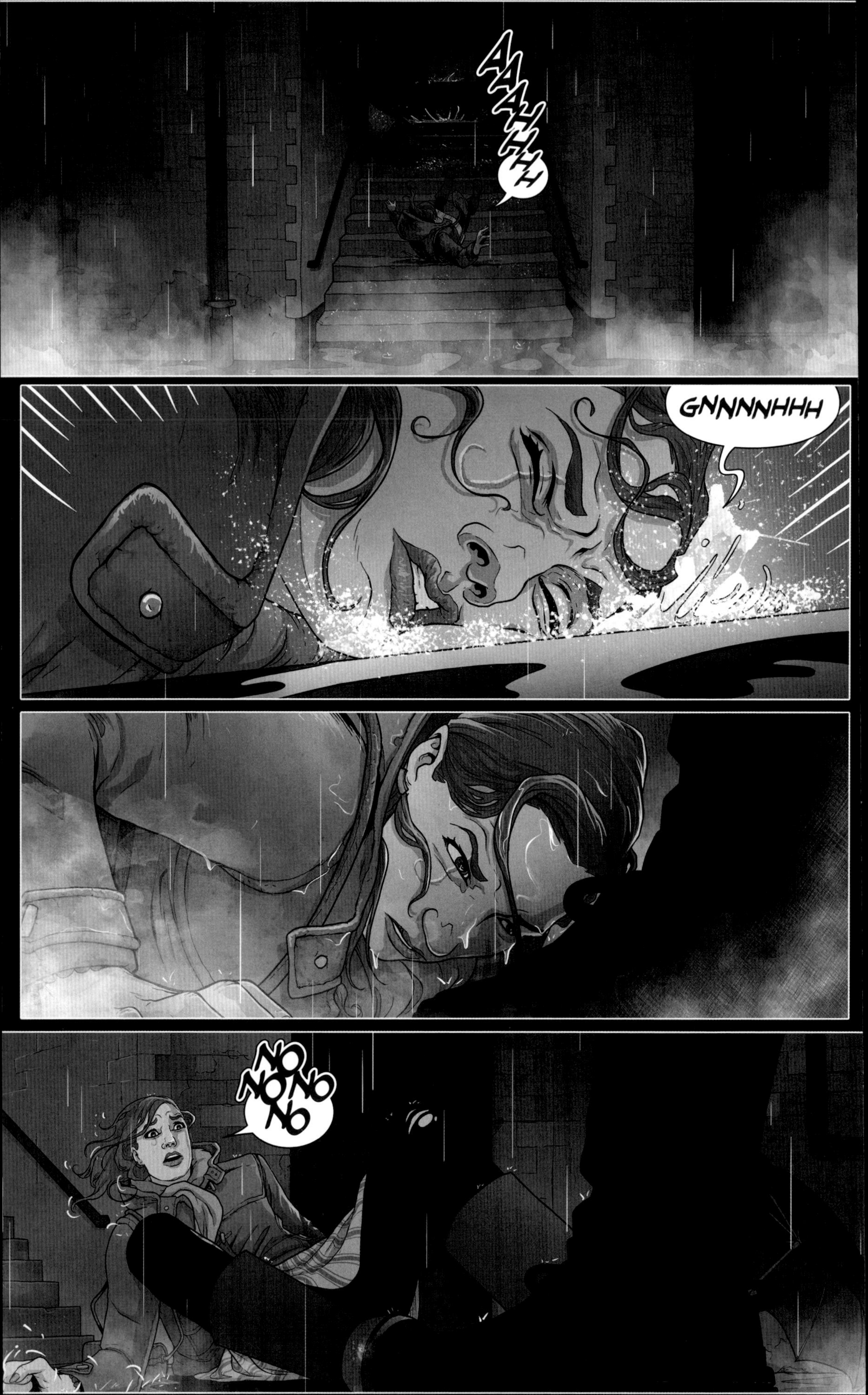
AAAAHHH
GNNNNHHH
NO NO NO NO

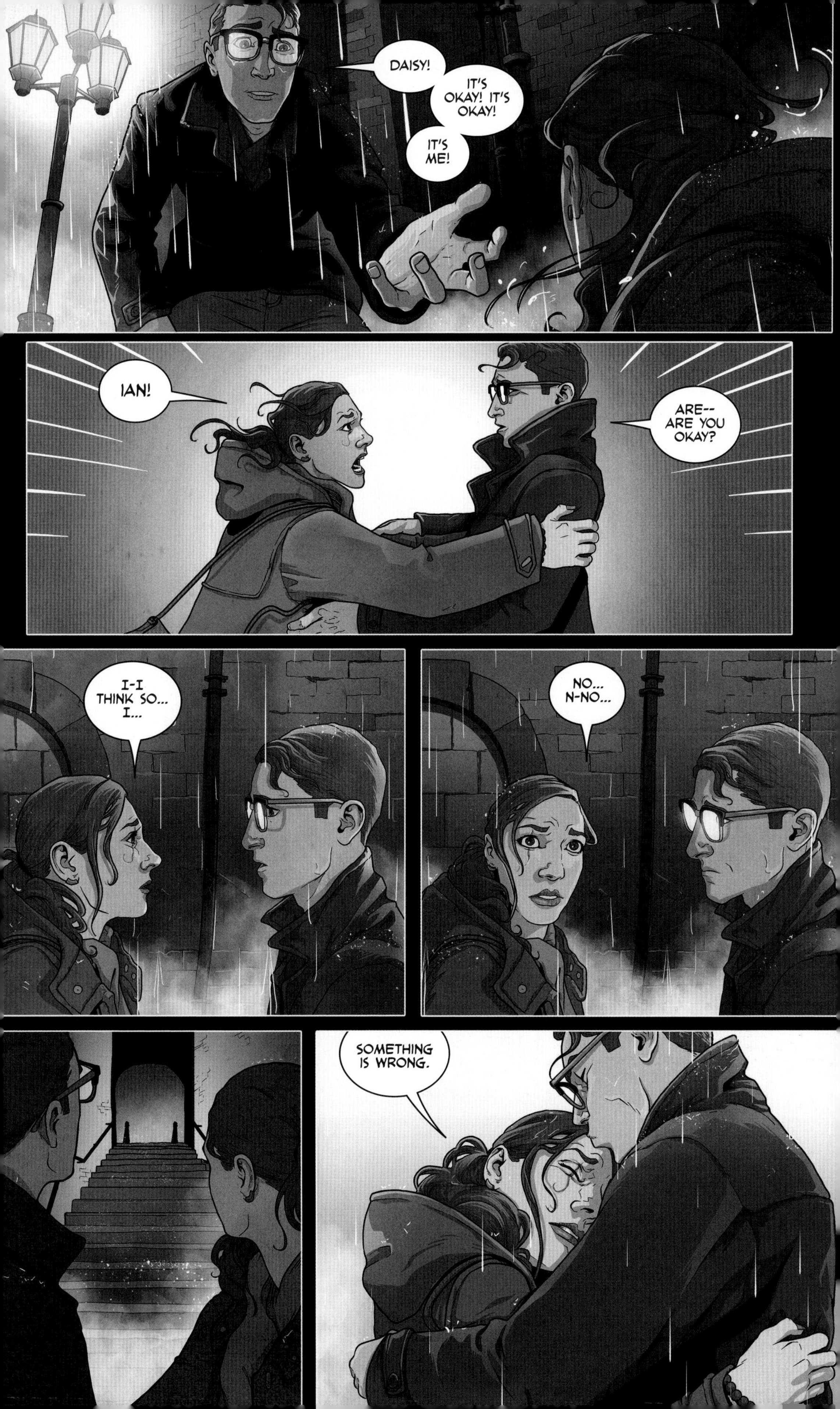
DAISY!
IT'S OKAY! IT'S OKAY!
IT'S ME!
IAN!
ARE-- ARE YOU OKAY?
I-I THINK SO... I...
NO... N-NO...
SOMETHING IS WRONG.

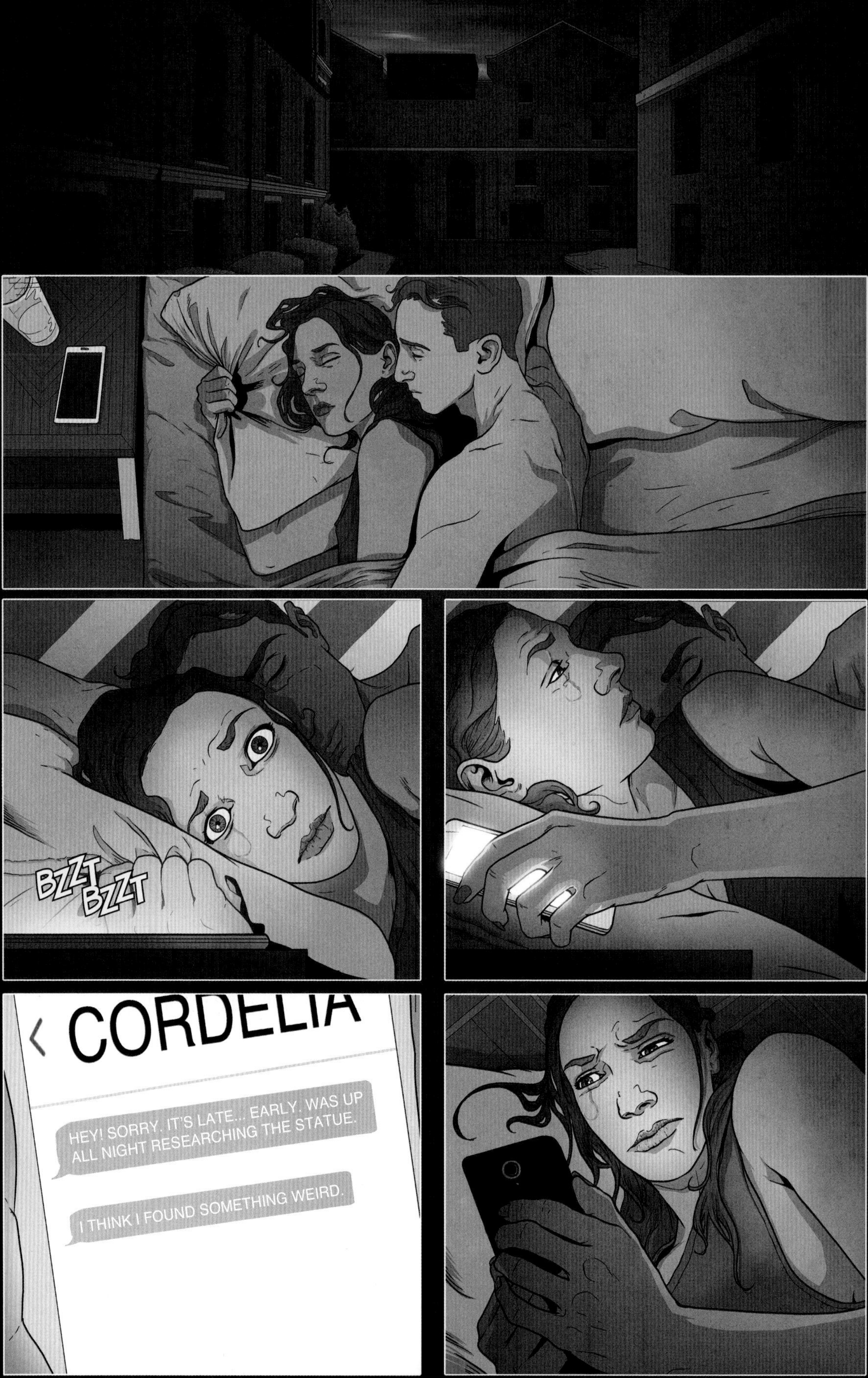
BZZT BZZT
CORDELIA
HEY! SORRY, IT'S LATE... EARLY. WAS UP ALL NIGHT RESEARCHING THE STATUE.
I THINK I FOUND SOMETHING WEIRD.

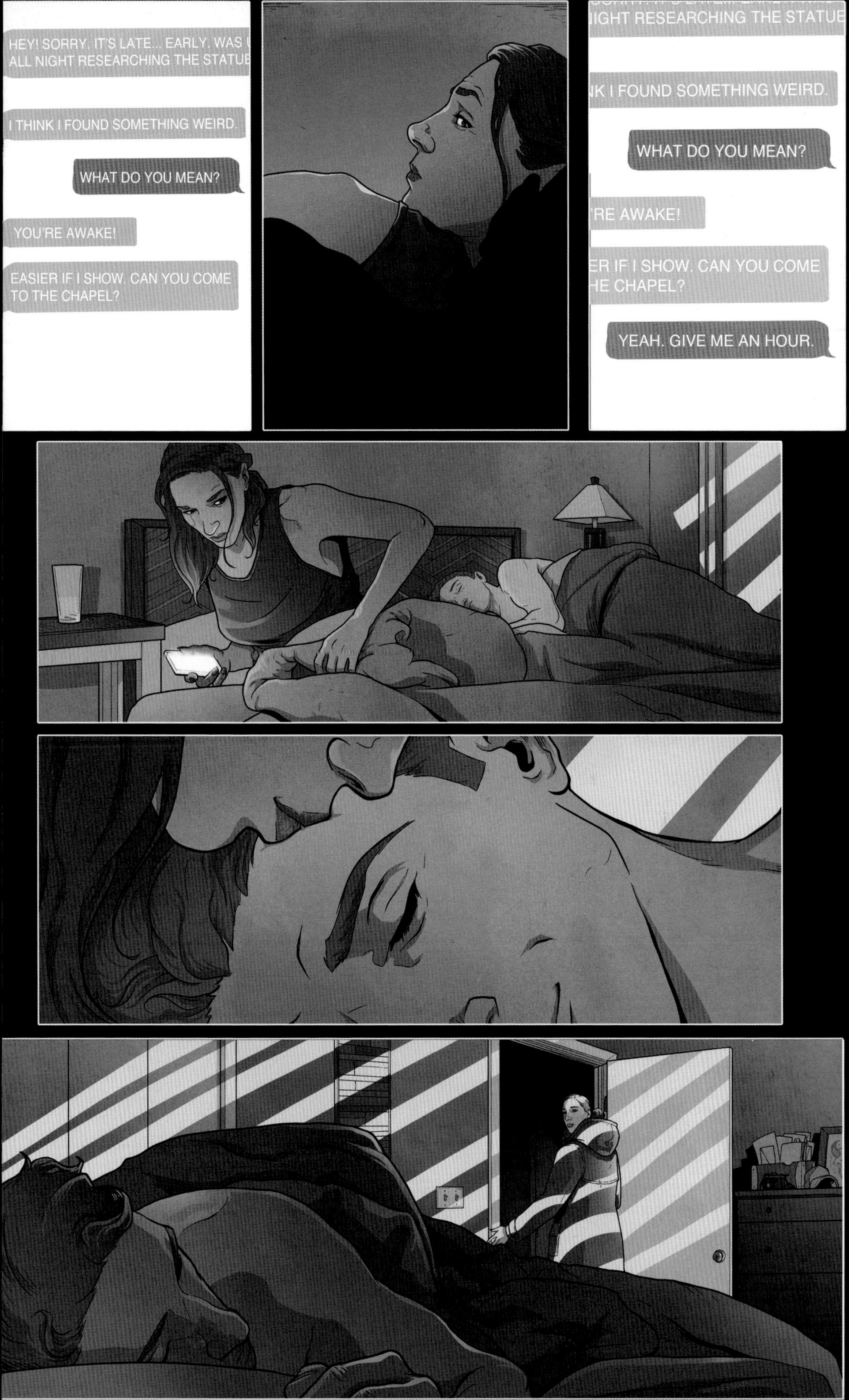
HEY! SORRY. IT'S LATE... EARLY. WAS
ALL NIGHT RESEARCHING THE STATUE
I THINK I FOUND SOMETHING WEIRD.
WHAT DO YOU MEAN?
YOU'RE AWAKE!
EASIER IF I SHOW. CAN YOU COME TO THE CHAPEL?
IGHT RESEARCHING THE STATUE
K I FOUND SOMETHING WEIRD.
WHAT DO YOU MEAN?
'RE AWAKE!
ER IF I SHOW. CAN YOU COME
HE CHAPEL?
YEAH. GIVE ME AN HOUR.

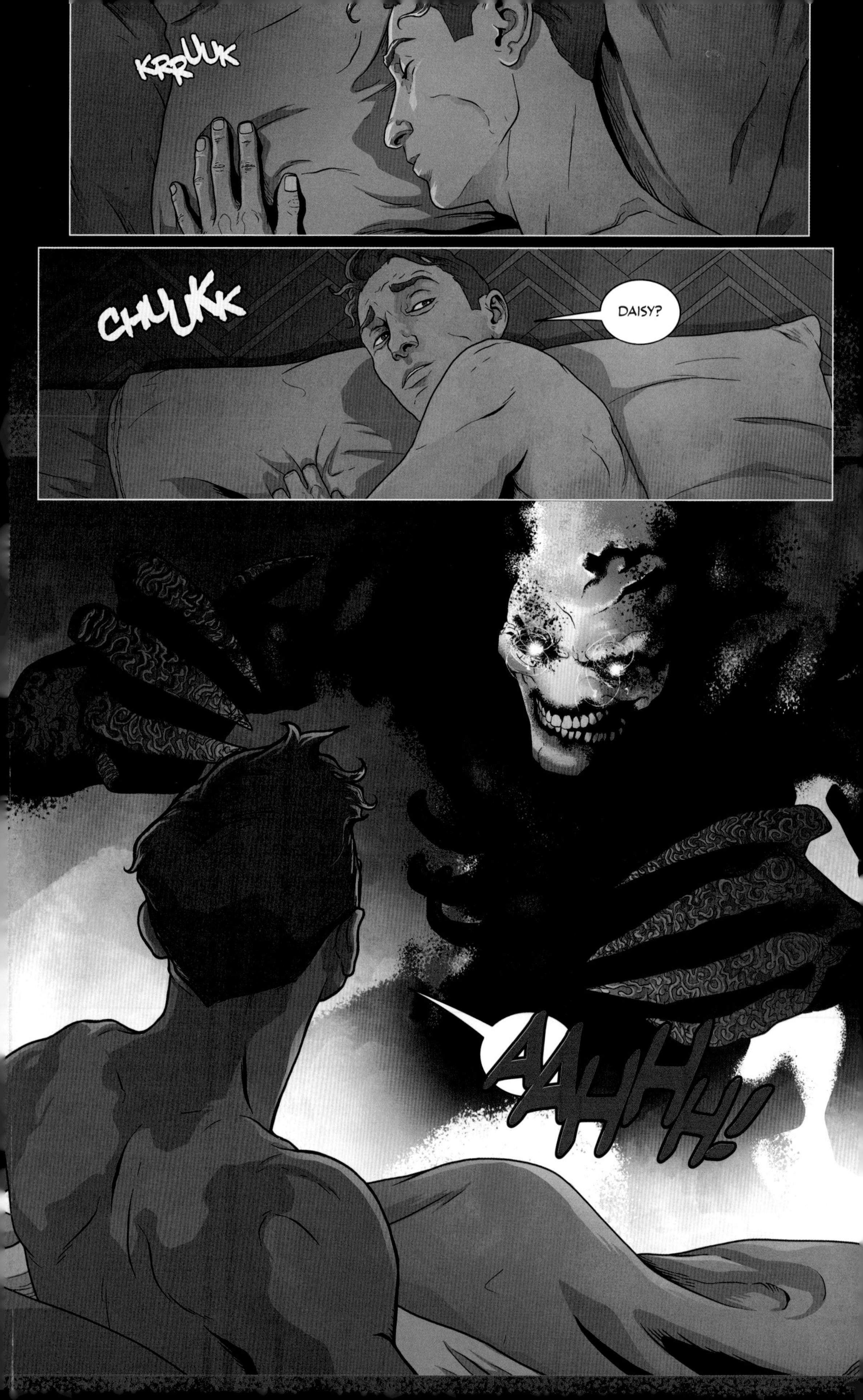
KRRUUK
CHUUKK
DAISY?
AAHHH!

TO BE CONTINUED...

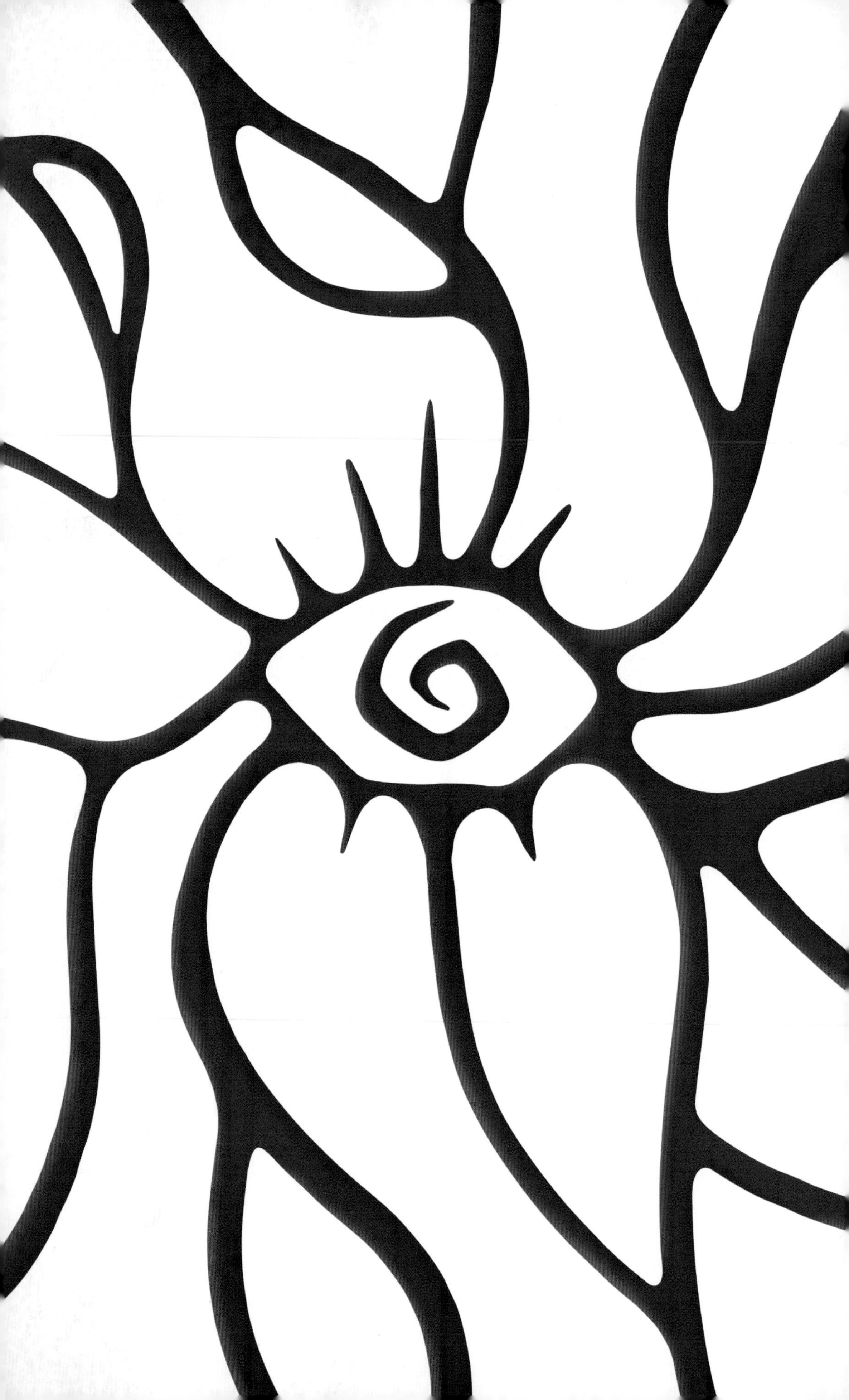

COVER
GALLERY

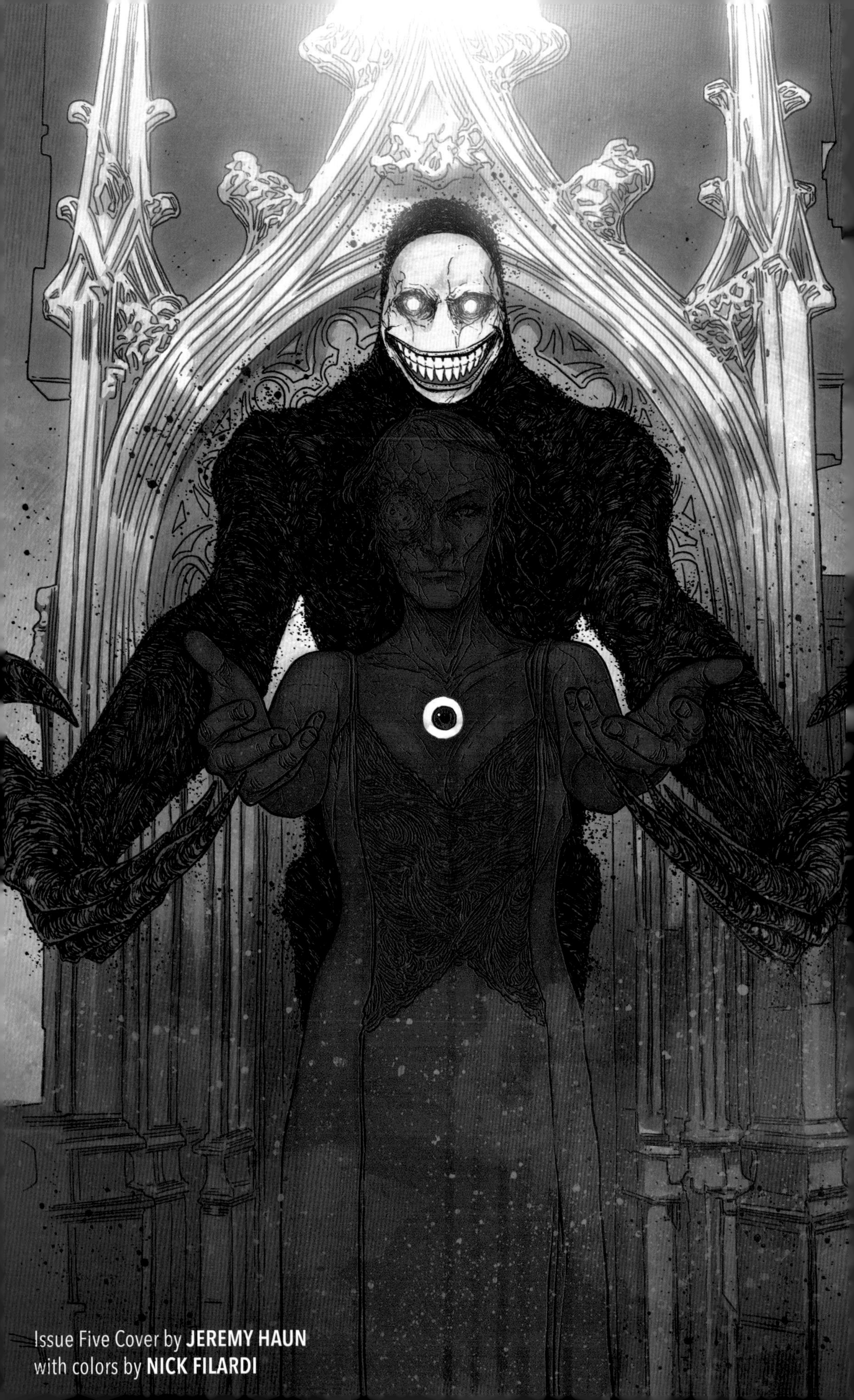

Issue Five Cover by **JEREMY HAUN**
with colors by **NICK FILARDI**

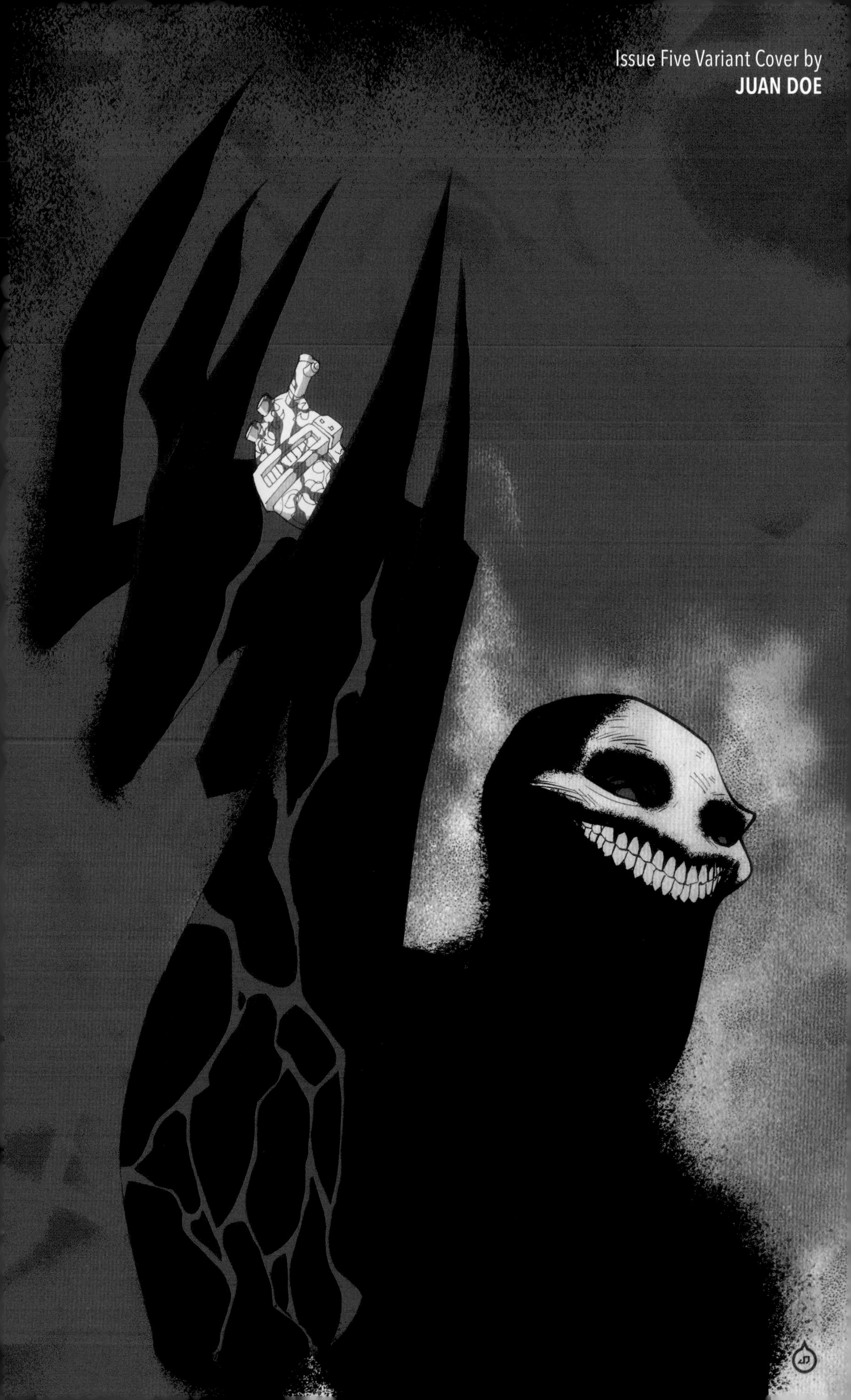

Issue Five Variant Cover by
JUAN DOE

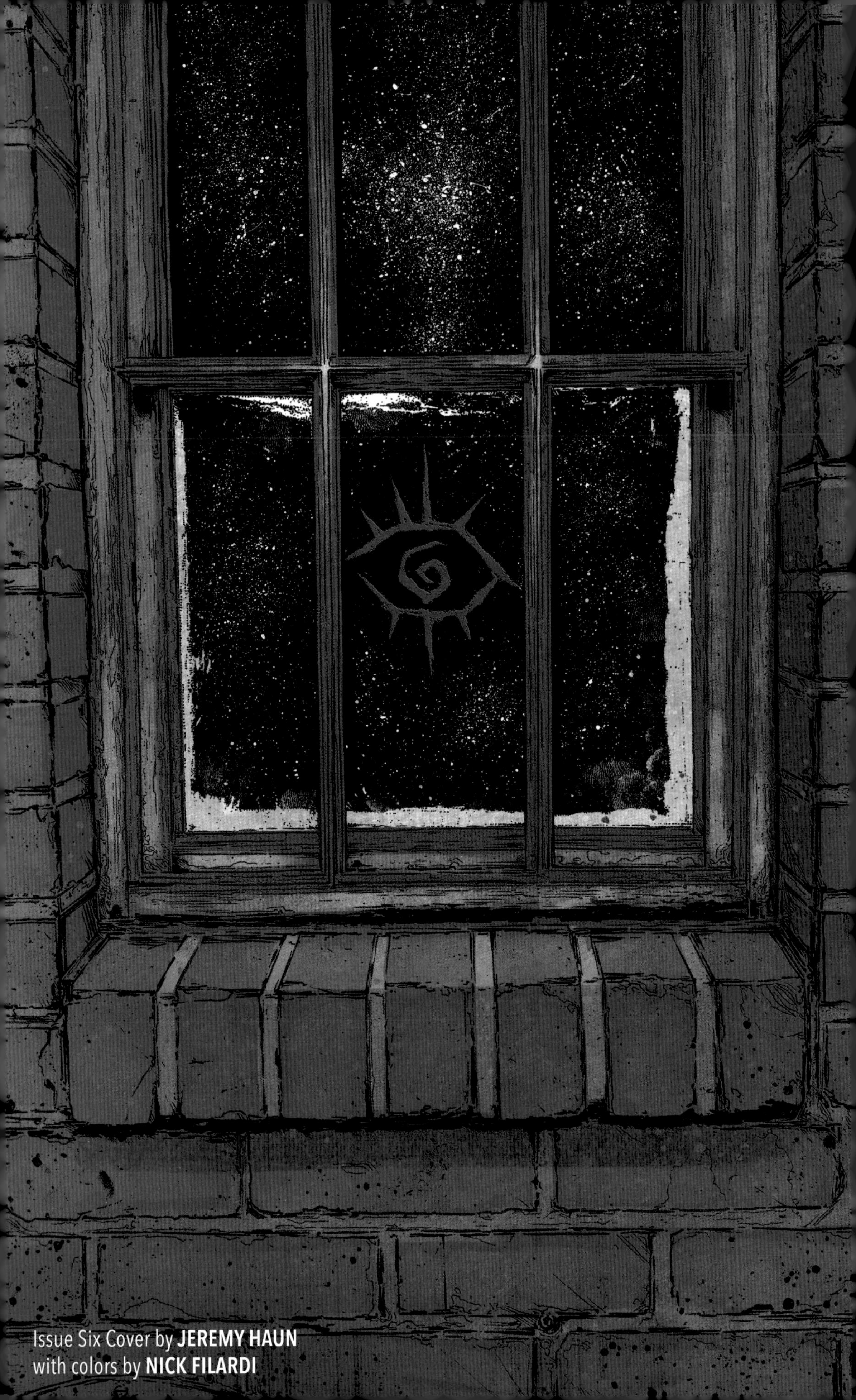

Issue Six Cover by **JEREMY HAUN**
with colors by **NICK FILARDI**

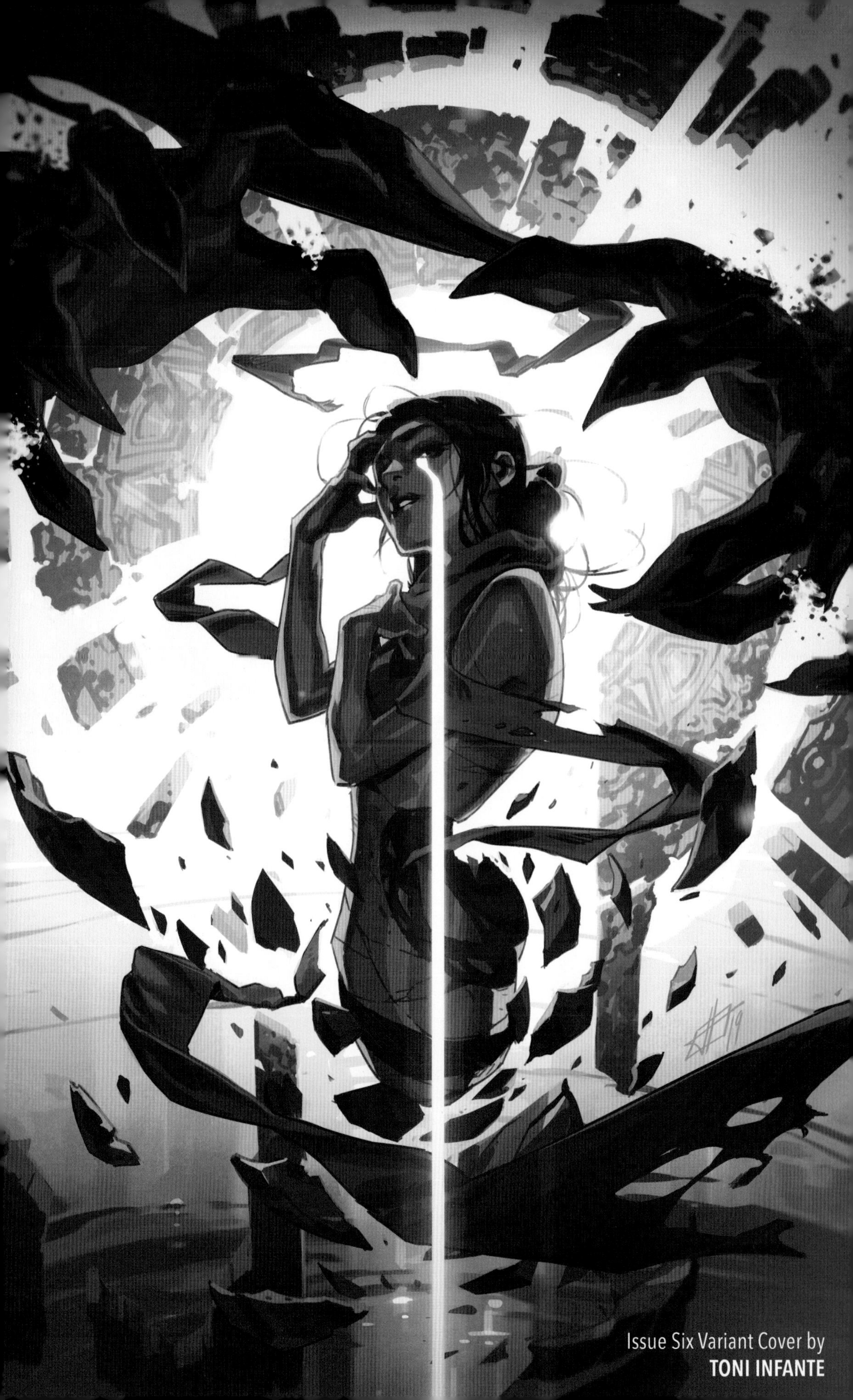

Issue Six Variant Cover by
TONI INFANTE

Issue Seven Cover by **JEREMY HAUN**
with colors by **NICK FILARDI**

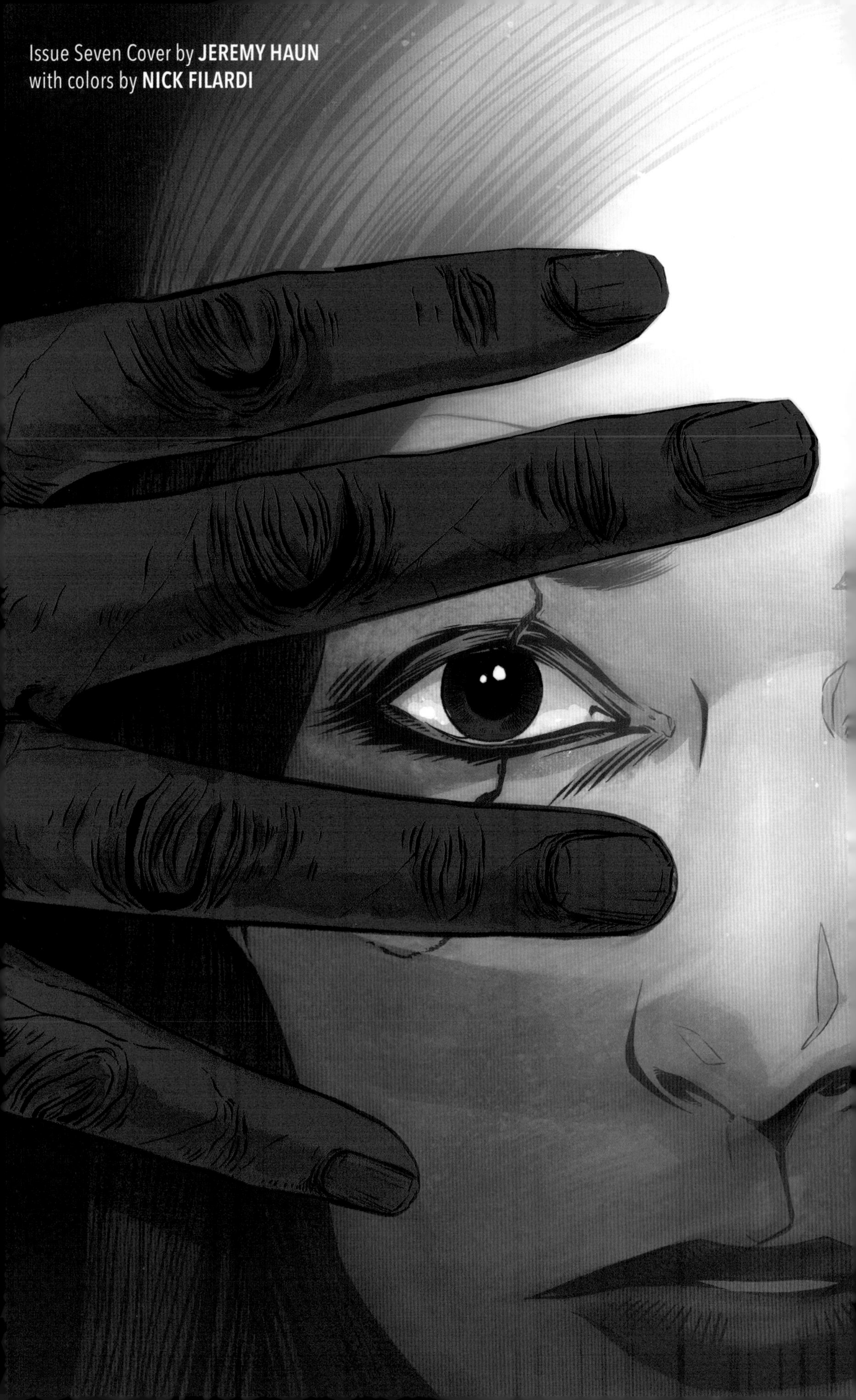

Issue Seven Variant Cover by
FRANY

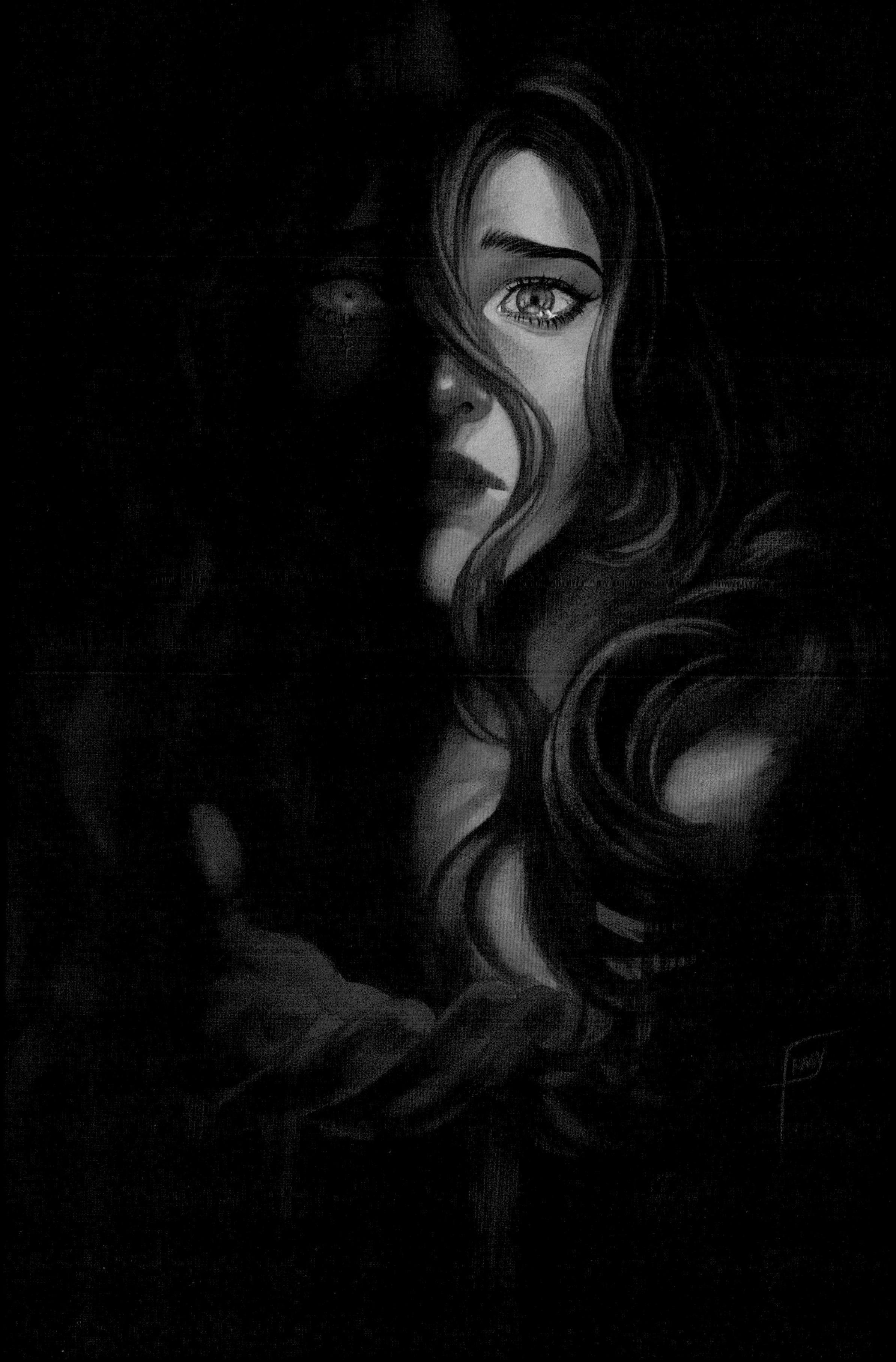

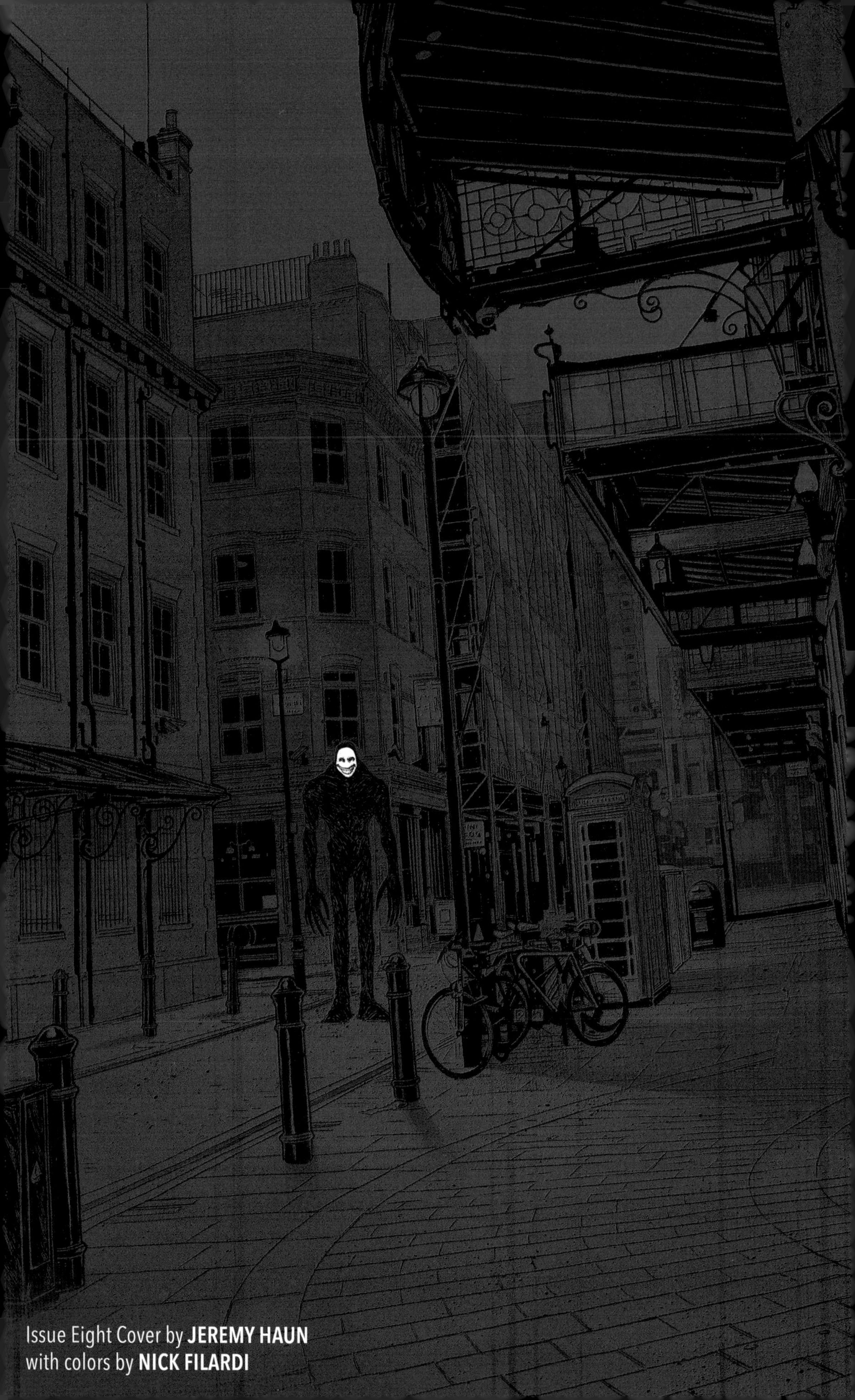

Issue Eight Cover by **JEREMY HAUN**
with colors by **NICK FILARDI**

Issue Eight Variant Cover by
JEREMY WILSON

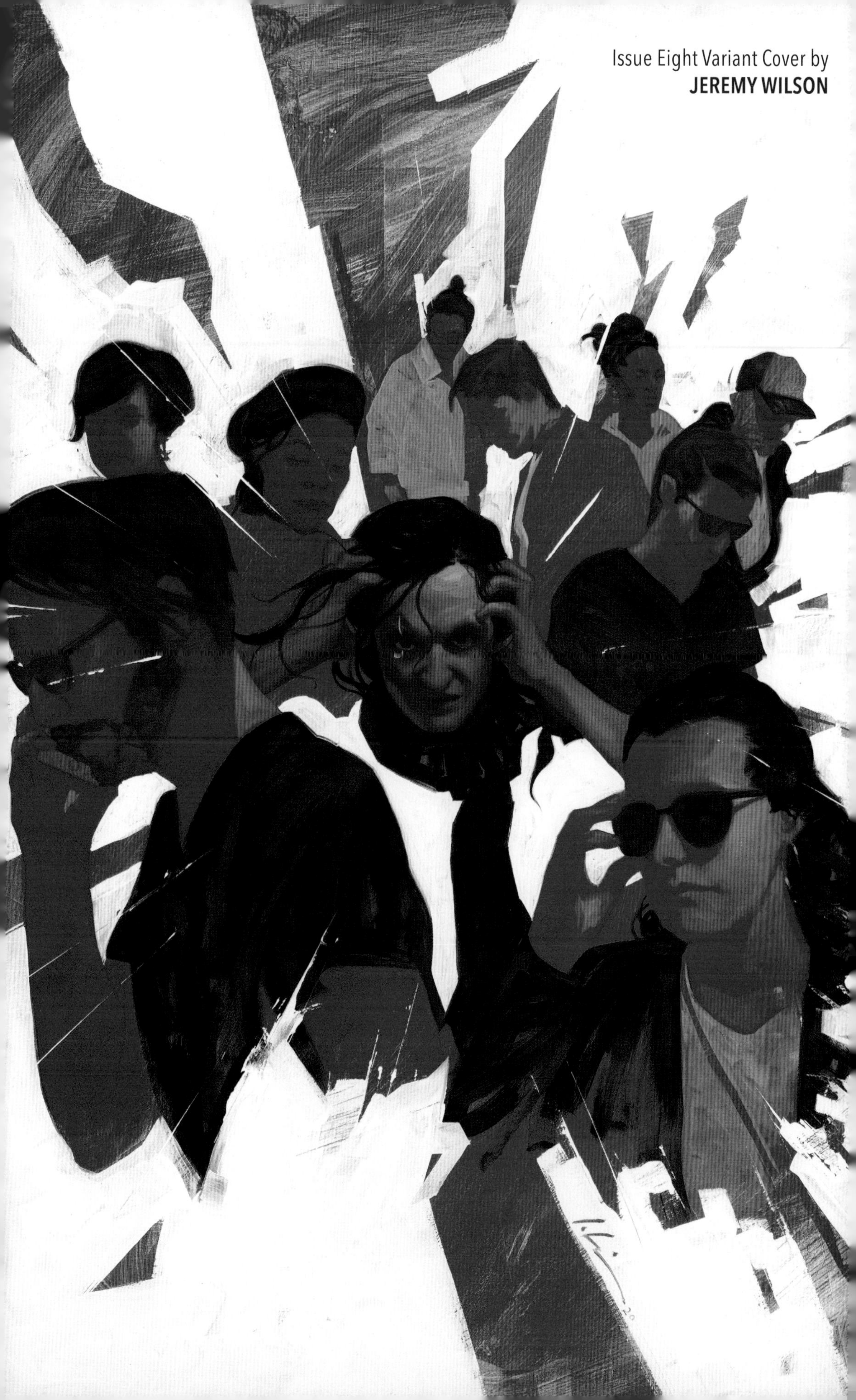

Additional Artwork by
DANNY LUCKERT

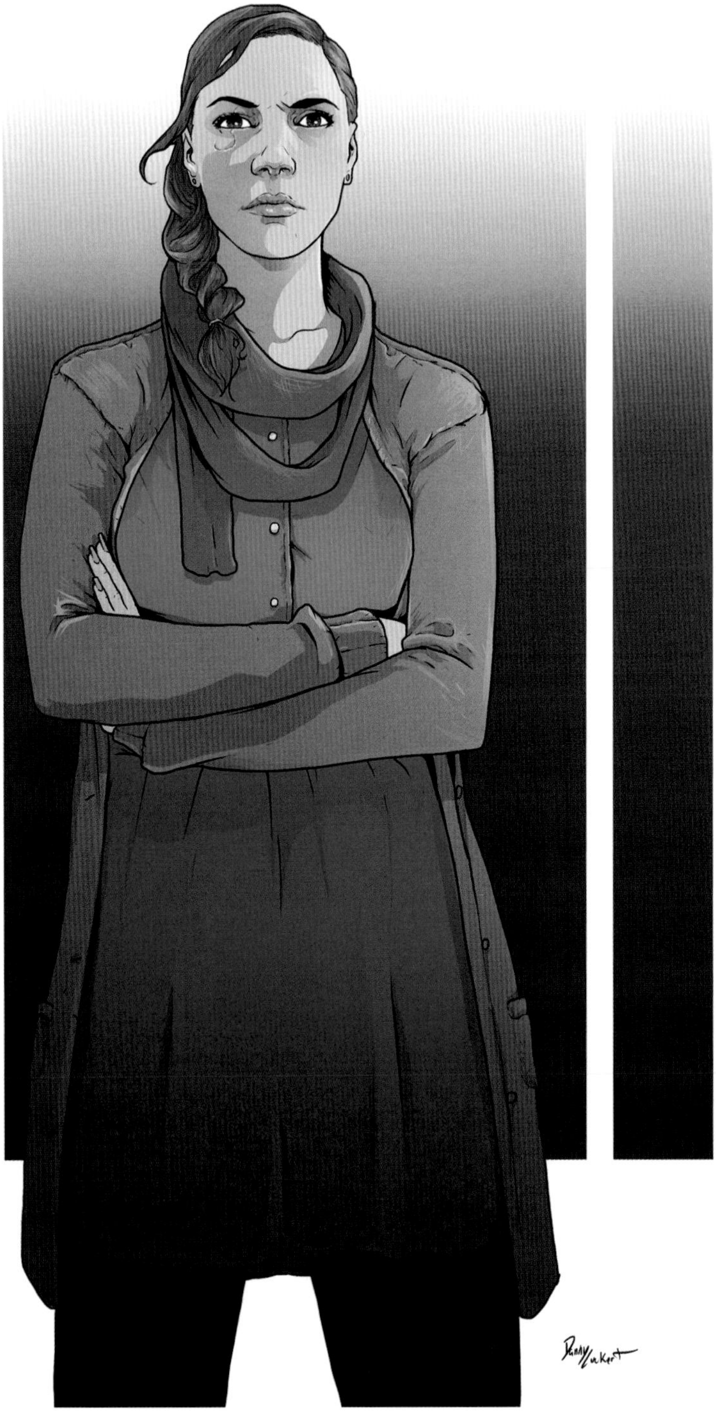

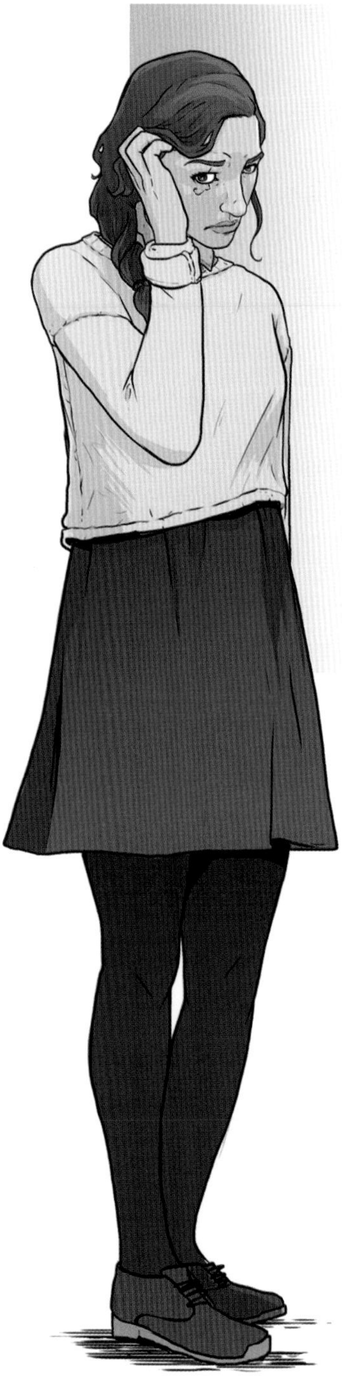

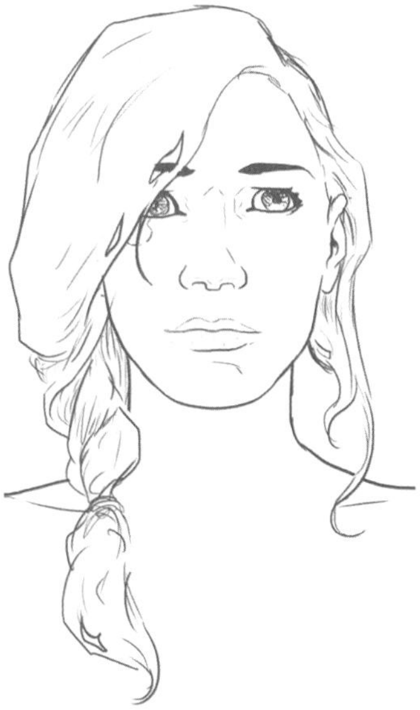

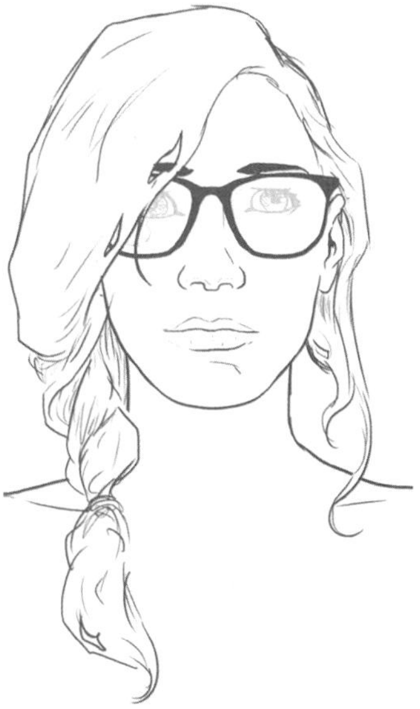

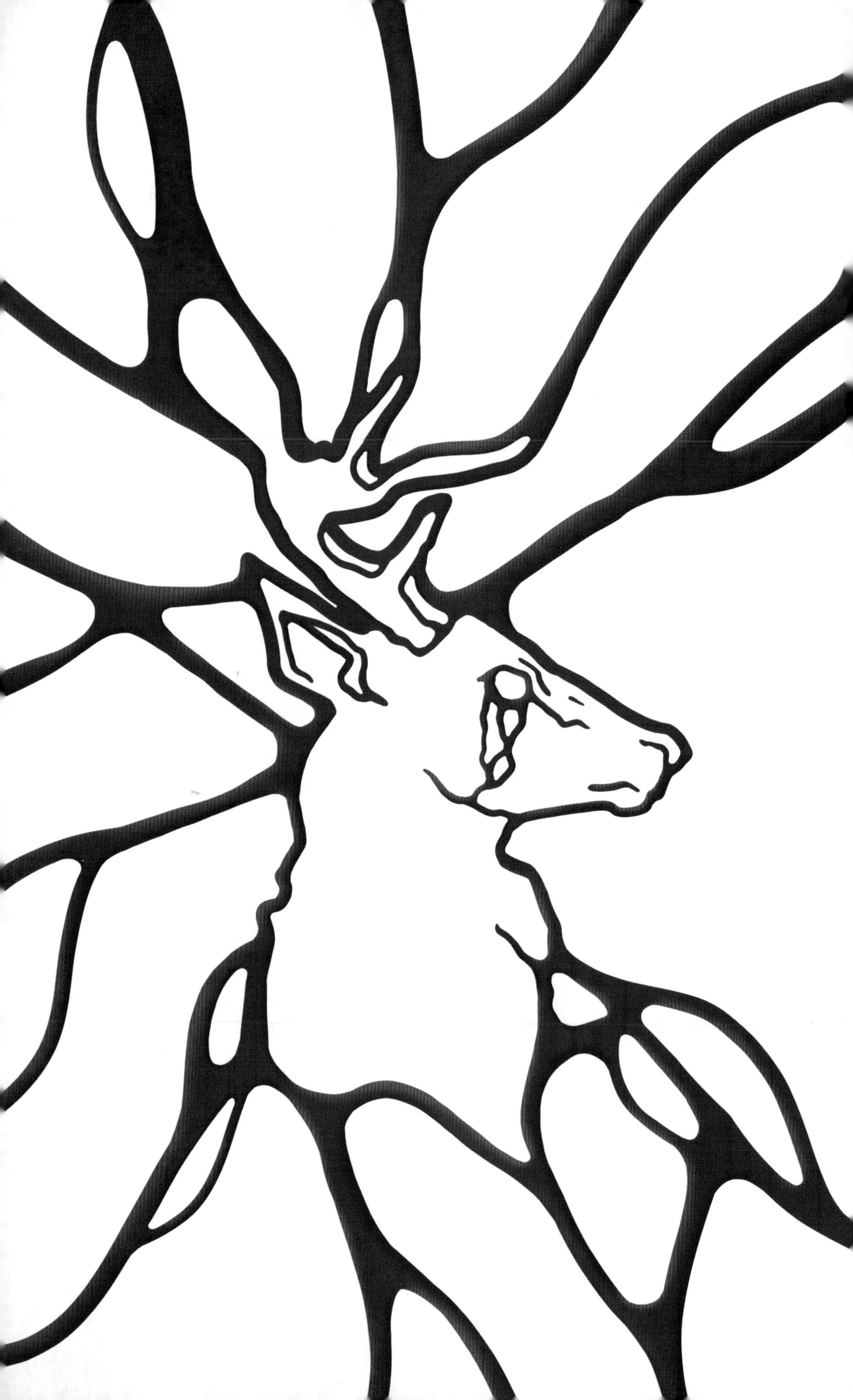